CONTENTS

CRAFTSTICKS, CUT-OUTS & DECOUPAGE
PAGE 35

PAPER FOLDS BOX AND CUT-OUTS
PAGE 43

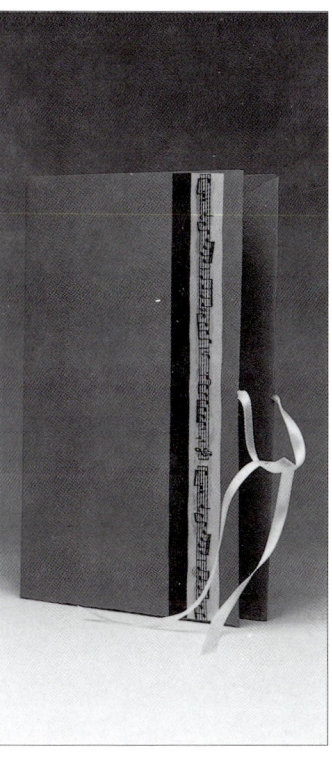

BEADS, LACE RIBBONS & PLASTIC
PAGE 51

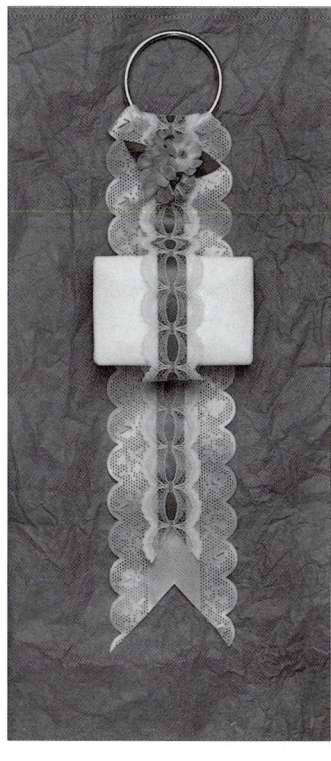

FABRIC PAINTS JARS & METALWORK
PAGE 65

Remote Control holder........ 35
Jail Bank................................36
Horse.....................................37
Mouse and Cheese................38
Pencil Holder........................39
Decorative Painting on Cutouts..............................40
Decoupage Christmas Plaque...................................41
Diamond Dust Ornament....42

Paper Folder......................... 43
Brown Bag Basket & Bows 44
Tissue Paper Flower............. 45
Paper Box..............................46
Paper Bird............................. 48
Paper Angel.......................... 49
Paper Snowflakes................. 50

Beaded Snowflake................ 51
Beaded Icicle......................... 52
Beaded Cartwheel Wreath...53
Bead & Lace Candy Cane... 54
Bead and Lace Heart............ 55
Bead and Lace Candle.......... 56
Lace Angel............................ 57
Ribbon Soap Holder............. 58
Ribbon and Feather Mask... 59
Woven Ribbon Barrette....... 60
Plastic Canvas Rainbow...... 61
Plastic Lacing Key Ring and Zipper Pull.................... 62
Plastic Canvas Jewelery Holder....................................64

T-Shirt Sponge Painting..........65
T-Shirt Masking tape Painting.....................................66
T-Shirt Fabric Stenciling.........67
Christmas Snowscene in a Jar 68
Snowman in a Jar....................69

GETTING

THINGS YOU NEED TO KNOW

Whether you are new to crafting or just looking for new ideas, you'll find "Projects for Kids" filled with wonderful things to make. These projects have been kid tested in our store and you'll find them fun, fast and easy to do. We've provided an approximate time, cost and skill level for each craft.

The cost given is for one finished project. This does not take into consideration you may have to buy a whole package of something in order to have just the one needed for the project. Ask at your local craft store if you can order supplies in bulk quantity to save money when working with large groups of children.

The time is an approximation of how long it should take an adult and child to complete one project for the first time. Allow extra time when you are working with more than one child.

Skill levels are given for each project to help you match up the projects with the kids. Projects should be challenging but not frustrating. When working with a group of children, do a sample project ahead of time to help you determine where extra help might be needed.

LEVEL 1 projects are fast and easy and have a minimum amount of preparation. The skills required are mainly cutting and gluing.

LEVEL 2 projects require a little more dexterity. They may be similar to level 1 projects but the materials may be smaller or the project may have more steps to it or take longer to complete.

LEVEL 3 projects have the most steps and require more time to complete. They will be the most challenging.

BE CREATIVE! Use the projects in this book to learn techniques and then have fun creating your own designs and projects. It's the fun that you and the children share while creating these projects that is the enjoyment of "Projects for Kids".

COPYRIGHT All rights reserved. No part of this book may be reproduced in any form without the written permission of the author, except by a reviewer who may quote brief passages in a magazine or newspaper when reviewing this publication.

DISCLAIMER The information in this book is presented in good faith but no warranty is given nor results guaranteed.

WARNING Due to the components used in this book, children under the age of eight years of age should not have access to the materials or supplies without adult supervision. Components or projects could cause serious or fatal injury. Neither Mark Publishing nor the supplier responsible for such injury.

STARTED

BASIC TOOLS YOU WILL NEED

Tacky glue is a water-based glue that dries clear. Because it is thick, it holds your project together while it dries. Do not use school glue unless you are gluing paper. Use tacky craft glue for felt, pom-poms, ribbon, beads, silk flowers, etc. Extra thick tacky craft glue is available for heavy or bulky materials. Note that craft glue must be allowed to completely dry between sessions, so allow more time than when using low heat glue gun.

Low heat
These electric glue guns allow you to assemble projects in minutes. The low heat makes working around children safer than if you were using a regular glue gun. You can still burn yourself, just not so severely, so use caution when working around children and teach them how to use one safely. You can do all the projects in this book without a glue gun, but the gun will save you time.

You will need a pair of craft scissors to cut wire, chenille stems, plastic and paper, and a pair of sharp scissors to cut ribbon, lace.

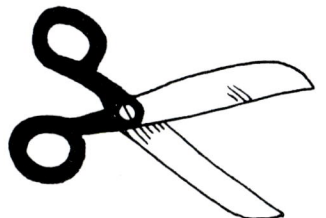

You will need wire cutters to cut heavy wire. You can also cut craft sticks with them.

HEY KIDS!

Before you get going, you should know that some of the projects in this book require help from an adult, especially those marked Level 3.

Once you set up your workshop in a spacious, brightly-lit area (kitchen tables are great, but be sure and ask someone first!), review the material list to make sure you have all the things you'll need for that project.

All the materials in this book can be found at your local craft store, but there may be times when you just can't find something. Don't worry - ask for help from a salesclerk. An alternative might be found just by wandering down a different aisle.

HAVE FUN!

CRAFT DESIGNER: Pat Roberts; COPY EDITOR: Bob Roberts
PHOTOGRAPHER: Todd Tsukushi; GRAPHIC DESIGN: Eagle Graphics
STYLIST: Allison Kelsen; INTERIOR DESIGNER: Randie Schneider

*Special thanks to **Jennifer Ziegenbein** for giving many of the projects in this book her "Kid's Seal of Approval".*

PINE CONE OWLS

Materials:
- 2 medium pine cones (small owl's body and large owl's head)
- 1 large pine cone (large owl's body)
- 1 small pine cone (small owl's head)
- 4 ea. 3" pieces of tan chenille stem (feet)
- 2 ea. 10 mm movable eyes (small owl's eyes)
- 2 ea. 14 mm movable eyes (large owl's eyes)
- a small branch for the owls to sit on
- 2"x 3" piece of black felt (eye patches)
- 24" light weight wire (hanger)
- extra thick tacky glue or low heat gun

1 Cut out the large and small eye patches from the black felt. Glue the eyes on top of the felt patches.

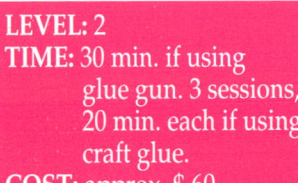

2 The flat end of the small pine cone will be the small owl's face. Lay this pine cone on its side on top of the flat end of a medium pine cone. Glue in place. To make the large owl, repeat this step with a medium and a large pine cone. Let the glue dry.

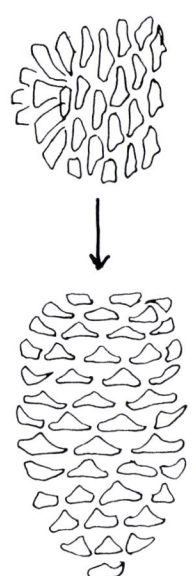

3 Break off six petals from an extra pine cone to make the beaks and ears. Trim two petals to form the beaks and glue them to the faces. Glue the eye patches to the faces. Glue the other four petals just above the eyes to form the ears. Let glue dry. Glue the owls to the branch.

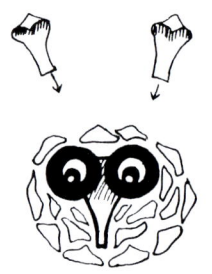

4 You may have to pull out a few petals from the owl bodies to make them fit onto the branch. Bend each of the chenille stems into the shape of the letter M to form the feet. Glue the feet to the bodies and bend them around the branch. Attach a light weight wire to the owls' heads to make a hanger.

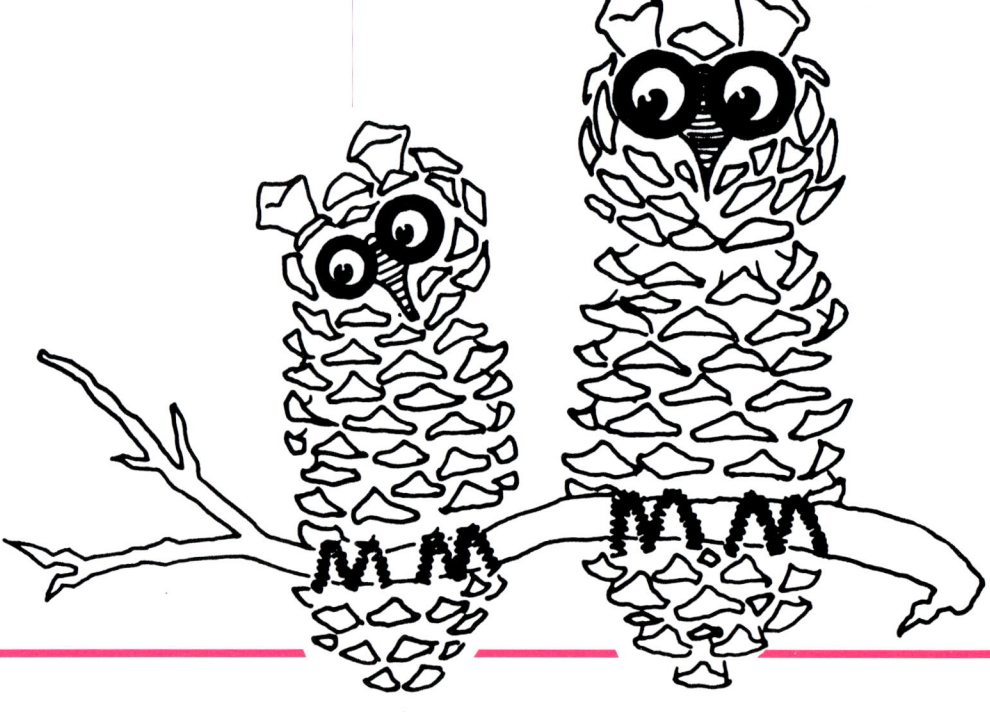

LEVEL: 2
TIME: 30 min. if using glue gun. 3 sessions, 20 min. each if using craft glue.
COST: approx. $.60

PINE CONE CHRISTMAS TREE

Materials:
1 ea. large pine cone
gold glitter
1 ea. gold star sequin
24 sequins, assorted colors and sizes
2 ea. 12" red tinsel stems
green spray paint
tacky craft glue

1 Spray paint the pine cone green. Let the paint dry completely.

2 Twist the tinsel stems together to make one long stem. Stick an end of a tinsel stem into the pine cone and wrap the tinsel stems around the cone to create a garland.

3 Glue glitter to the outer edges of the pine cone. Glue sequins to the pine cone to make ornaments.

4 Glue a star sequin to the top of the pine cone.

Simple projects like these are a great way to get started. You'll love the results!

LEVEL: 1
TIME: 2 sessions, 10 min. each
COST: approx. $.75

PINE CONE ORNAMENT

Materials:
- 1 ea. large pine cone
- 12" length of 1/8" ribbon
- small dried and silk flowers
- gloss acrylic spray
- tacky craft glue
- small feathered bird

1. Break several pieces off the wide side of the pine cone to make it flat.

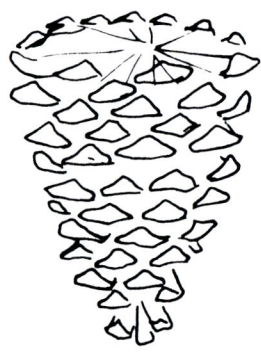

2. Separate the dried flowers into several small bunches and glue them to the wide end of the cone. Glue in a few small silk flowers. Glue the bird down into the middle of the dried flowers. Glue one end of the ribbon into the cone about one inch below the dried flowers.

3. Bring the end of the ribbon up and over the cone to the opposite side. Glue this end to the cone on the same level as the other side.

4. Spray the cone with a light coat of gloss spray.

What a beautiful ornament you can create in just minutes! Your Christmas tree will take on a whole new look.

LEVEL: 1
TIME: 20 min.
COST: approx. $1.50

PINE CONE TURKEY

Materials:
1 ea. large pine cone
1 ea. 3" orange bump chenille
2 ea. 7 mm movable eyes
6-10 ea. 5" feathers (assorted colors)
2 ea. 2" pieces of orange chenille stem
1" square red felt
tacky craft glue

1 Cut out the wattle from the red felt.

2 Lay the pine cone on its side. The narrow end will be the front of the turkey. Bend the bump chenille to form the turkey's head and neck. Glue the neck down into the front end of the pine cone.

3 Glue the eyes to the turkey's head. Glue the wattle onto the turkey's beak. Glue the feathers to the backside of the pine cone to make the turkey's tail.

4 Bend both pieces of chenille stem into the shape of the letter M. Glue the stems to the bottom of the turkey to make the feet.

LEVEL: 1
TIME: 20 min.
COST: approx. $.50

STRAW HAT

Materials:
1 ea. 4" to 6" wide straw hat
small bunches of dried flowers
assorted tiny silk flowers
2 ea. 12" lengths of narrow ribbon, two colors
1 ea. 14" length of 7/8" ribbon
2 small pieces of light weight wire
tacky craft glue

1 Tie a quick bow with the 7/8" ribbon and a piece of wire. Directions for making a quick bow are given below.

2 Cut the narrow ribbons in half and glue them to the brim of the hat to create the streamers. Glue the bow on top of the streamers.

3 Break the dried flowers up into small bunches and glue them to the hat on either side of the bow. Hide the dried flower stems up under the bow. Trim the stems of the silk flowers to 1/2" and glue them down into the dried flowers.

4 Bend the second piece of wire into a loop and glue it to the back of the hat to form a hanger.

QUICK BOW

Materials:
Small bow: 6" length of 1/8" ribbon
            4" length of light weight wire
Medium bow: 12" length of 7/8" ribbon
            6" length of light weight wire
Large bow: 16" length of 1-1/2" ribbon
            6" length of light weight wire

1 Trim the ends of the ribbon at an angle.

2 Lay out the ribbon in front of you with the wrong side facing up.

3 Criss-cross the two ends of the ribbon to form a loop. Pinch the center of the loop to form the bow.

4 Wrap the wire around the center of the bow and twist the ends together at the back of the bow.

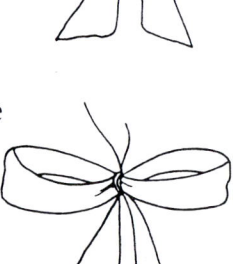

LEVEL: 2
TIME: 20 min.
COST: approx. $1.50

POTPOURRI BASKET

Materials:
1 ea. 3" wood chip basket
12" length of 1/4" ribbon
2 Tbsp. potpourri
2 small silk flowers
10" length of metallic thread
tacky craft glue

1 Cut and glue the ribbon onto the handle and outer rim of the basket.

2 Crumble the potpourri into small pieces. Cover the sides of the basket with an even coating of tacky craft glue. Press the potpourri into the glue.

3 Glue a small silk flower to each side of the handle. Attach the metallic thread to the handle to make a hanger.

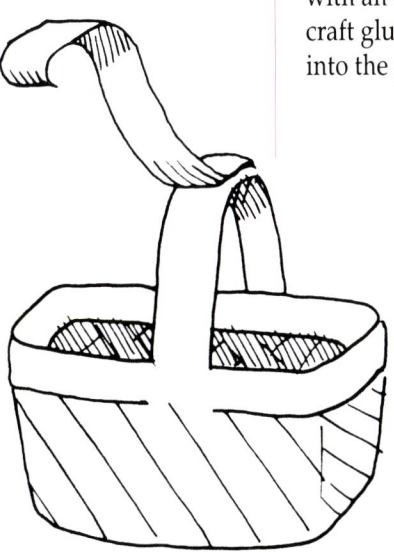

This not only makes a great Christmas tree ornament, but could be used at Easter to display that special Easter egg!

LEVEL: 1
TIME: 20 min.
COST: approx. $1.00

SACHET

Materials:
- 10" length of 3" ribbon
- 12" length of 1/8" ribbon
- small silk flowers, assorted colors
- potpourri oil or candle scent
- cotton balls
- tacky craft glue or a low heat glue gun

1 Make a fold across the 3" ribbon about 4" from one end as shown.

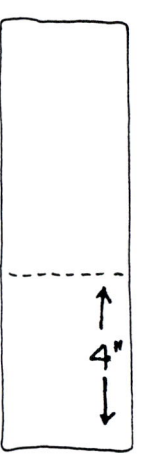

2 Match up the edges. Glue the edges together to form a pocket. Let glue dry.

3 Place a little potpourri oil on a cotton ball. To keep the oil from staining the outside of the sachet, wrap the oil soaked cotton ball up inside a couple of cotton balls that you have pulled apart and place them inside the pocket. Lay the 1/8" ribbon across the opening of the pocket.

4 Fold the end of the 3" ribbon into a point and glue it down to seal up the pocket. Bring up the ends of the 1/8" ribbon and tie them together to make a loop.

5 Glue the silk flowers and a couple of leaves to the front of the sachet. Use the loop to hang the sachet from a door knob or a hanger. If you use Christmas ribbon for the sachet, substitute small plastic holly for the silk flowers. Use cinnamon or pine scent for holiday sachets.

LEVEL: 1
TIME: 20 min. if using glue gun
2 sessions, 20 min. each if using craft glue
COST: approx. $1.00

WOODEN BEAD VASE

Materials:
1 ea. 40 mm wooden bead
small bunch of dried flowers
assorted tiny silk flowers
tacky craft glue

1. Squeeze some glue into the hole of the bead. Push the stems of the dried flowers down into the hole.

2. Cut the stems of the silk flowers 1" long. Put glue on the stems of the flowers and glue them into the bead.

What a terrific dollhouse accessory this makes! Watch the face of the little girl who makes it herself, or the one who receives it as a gift!

LEVEL: 1
TIME: 10 min.
COST: approx. $.75

WHEAT WEAVING HEART

Materials:
18 pieces of wheat
36" length of strong thread or embroidery floss
12" length of 7/8" ribbon
6" length of light weigth wire

1 Break off the straw just above the joint and slide the leaf off each of the eighteen pieces of wheat. The joint is the dark ring near the bottom of the straw. Soak the wheat in water for 30 minutes to make the wheat easy to work with.

2 Tie the pieces of wheat together just under the heads. Tie another knot around the wheat about 3" from the first knot.

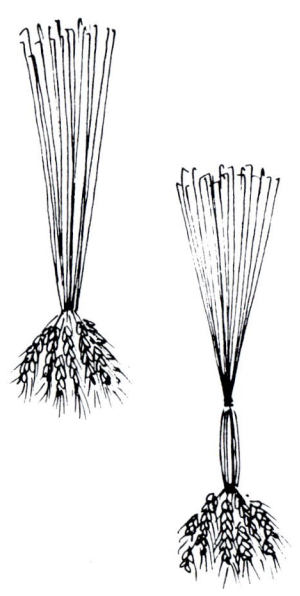

3 Divide the straws into two groups of nine. Take one of these groups and divide it into three groups of three straws. Braid these three groups for seven inches and tie a knot at the bottom of the braid and trim the straws 1" from the knot.

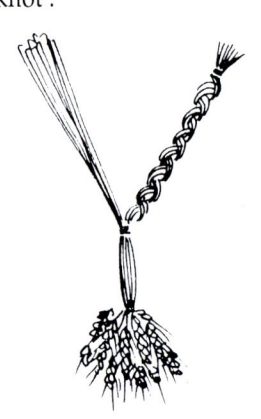

4 Divide the remaining nine straws into three groups of three straws and braid this group for seven inches. Trim the ends. Bend the two braids down to form the sides of the heart.

5 Tie the braids to the base of the wheat heads. Lay the heart flat to dry. Make a quick bow with the ribbon and wire and attach it to the heart after the wheat is dry. Directions for making quick bows are given in this book. Do not leave wet wheat in a plastic bag or it will sprout. Do not leave wheat out where your pets can reach it. They may eat it!

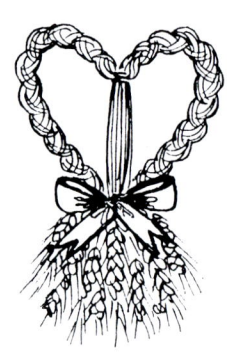

LEVEL: 2
TIME: 30 min. to soak wheat, 30 mins. for project
COST: approx. $1.10

PUPPY PUPPET

Materials:
9" x 12" piece of tan long fake fur
6" sq. piece of brown long fake fur
1 pair of 21 mm brown animal eyes
1 ea. 25 mm animal nose
5" x 9" piece of pink felt
2" x 4" piece of brown felt
needle and thread
glue (see page 3)

1 Fold the piece of tan fur, fur side facing in, in half lengthwise. From the back of the fabric, cut a 5" slit down along the fold. When cutting long fake fur, always cut from the back side and take short snips with the tips of the scissors. This will allow you to cut just the backing and not cut through the long hair along the edge of the cut.

2 Trim the corners to make them round. Trim one of the rounded ends about 1" shorter than the other. The short end is the puppy's lower jaw. The longer end is the puppy's face.

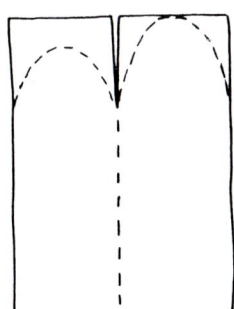

3 With the fur still folded in half, fur side in, stitch up the edges of the fur.

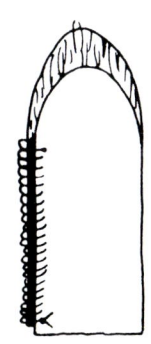

4 Snip small slits in the longer piece where you want the eyes, nose and ears to go. Attach the eyes and nose. Turn the puppy right side out.

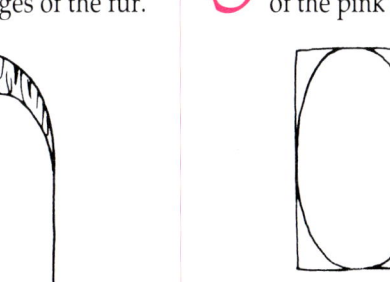

5 Open the puppy's mouth. Trim the corners of the pink felt.

6 Place glue all around the inside edge of the puppy's mouth and press the pink felt down on top of the glue. After the glue has dried, trim off the excess felt along the edge of the mouth.

7 Cut out the ears from the brown fur and push the small ends of the ears down through the small slits on the top of the head. Glue or stitch the ends of the ears in place inside the puppy.

8 Cut out the tongue from the brown felt and glue it inside the puppy's mouth.

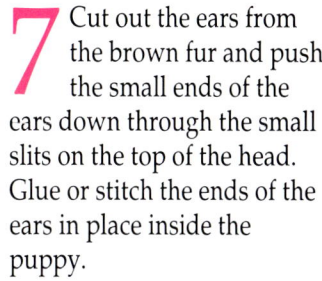

LEVEL: 3
TIME: 2 sessions, 40 min. each using tacky craft glue
60 min. using glue gun
COST: $ 4.00

MOP DOLL

Materials:
- 1 ea. 8 oz. cotton mop head
- 1 ea. 2" styrofoam ball
- 1 ea. 12" x 18" piece of cotton muslin
- 1 ea. 5" straw hat
- 36" length of strong string
- low heat glue gun or extra thick tacky craft glue
- 2 ea. 4 mm half round beads
- fine line black permanent marker
- powdered rouge

1. Wrap one end of the cotton muslin around the styrofoam ball, keeping the muslin as free of wrinkles as you possibly can. Tie a knot under the ball with a piece of the string. This makes the doll's head.

2. Pull out four strings from the mop to be used for hair. Cut one of the strings into 2" pieces and the other three strings into 4" pieces. Glue the 2" pieces about 1/2" up inside the hat. These pieces should be side by side. They are the doll's bangs.

3. Glue the 4" pieces to the inside of the hat. They also should be 1/2" up inside the hat and side by side. They are the rest of the doll's hair. After the glue has completely dried, untwist mop strands to fill out the hair.

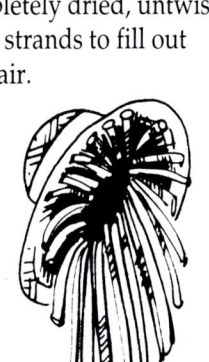

4. At one end of the mop count out fifteen strands on each side of the mop ribbon. Divide one of the groups of fifteen strands into three groups of five and tie a tight braid for 4 1/2". Tie off the braid with a piece of the string. Trim the strands 1" from the knot. Untwist the ends. This makes an arm. Repeat for the other group of fifteen strands to make the other arm.

5. Place the head on top of the mop and position it so that the neck is even with the arms. Fold under the raw edges of the fabric and anchor the fabric to the mop ribbon with a little glue. The long end of the fabric is the doll's apron.

6 Pick up three strands from each side of the mop ribbon, just under the arms. Criss cross these pieces up and over the shoulders. Let them hang straight down the doll's back.

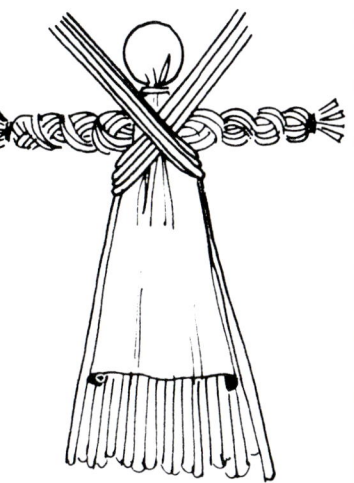

7 Pick up two strands from each side of the mop ribbon on the back side of the doll and bring them around to the front, criss crossing at the front. Bring them around to the back and tie them together in a tight bow.

BACK

8 Hide the mop ribbon by gluing some strands to it in the front and back of the doll. Glue the hat onto the head. Trim the bangs and hair if needed.

9 Glue the beads to the face. Draw a smile and freckles with the permanent pen. Brush on a little powdered rouge to the doll's cheeks.

10 You can tie knots in some of the dress strands and tie little bows to the knots. Glue little silk flowers to the hat or glue a basket to the doll's hands if you wish.

LEVEL: 3
TIME: 60 min.
COST: $ 4.00

RAFFIA DOLL

Materials:
1 ea. 38 mm wood bead
10" length of 16 g wire
2 oz. of raffia

1 Cut some of the raffia into fifty 24" long pieces. Form a bundle with the pieces and tie them in the middle with a piece of raffia. Be careful not to pull this piece of raffia too tight because it will break.

2 Count out ten pieces of raffia on both sides of the knot and thread these pieces through the hole in the wood bead. Pull the rest of the raffia in the bundle down around the bead to form the hair. Tie a piece of raffia around the entire bundle under the bead to create the neck.

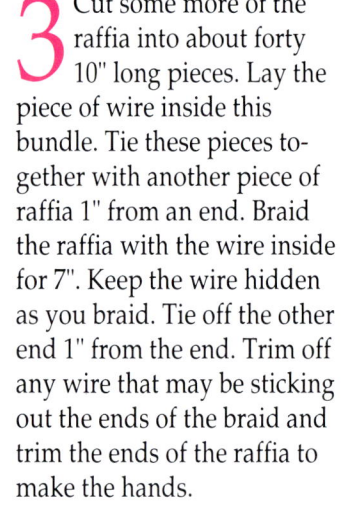

3 Cut some more of the raffia into about forty 10" long pieces. Lay the piece of wire inside this bundle. Tie these pieces together with another piece of raffia 1" from an end. Braid the raffia with the wire inside for 7". Keep the wire hidden as you braid. Tie off the other end 1" from the end. Trim off any wire that may be sticking out the ends of the braid and trim the ends of the raffia to make the hands.

4 Divide the main bundle of raffia just below the neck into a front and a back group. Slide the arms up between these two groups. Tie a piece of raffia around the entire bundle to make the waist.

5 Make two bundles of 20" long pieces of the remaining raffia. Drape a bundle over each shoulder and tie them at the waist. Trim the bottom of the dress and pose the arms. Spread the dress out slightly to make the doll stand up.

LEVEL: 2
TIME: 30 min.
COST: $ 1.75

SOFT SCULPTURE LEPRECHAUN

Materials:
- 3" sq. piece of ivory colored nylon stocking
- polyester fiber-fil
- needle and white thread
- 2 ea. 4 mm black beads
- 1 ea. 35 mm black top hat
- small piece of brown fiber or yarn for hair
- 4" length of 5/8" green satin ribbon
- 2-1/2" x 5" piece of green felt
- 2" sq. piece of light pink felt
- 1 ea. 2-1/2" styrofoam ball
- 6" piece of black chenille stem
- gold glitter
- black acrylic paint
- powdered blush
- glue (see page 3)

1 Cut the piece of stocking into a 3" circle. With the needle and about 24" of thread, make a row of running stitches around the circle, about 1/4" from the edge.

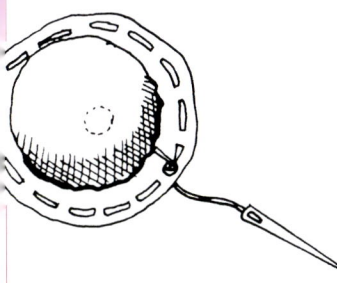

2 Place a little pea sized piece of poly-fil in the middle of the stocking, followed by a larger ball of poly-fil on top of it.

3 Gather the stitches up around the ball of poly-fil by pulling up on the needle and thread. Tie a couple of knots to hold the gathered stitches in place. Push the needle from the back through the poly-fil to the front. Have the needle come out the front next to the small piece of poly-fil. Gently pull the small piece of poly-fil away from the head to create the nose. Wrap the thread around the nose a couple of times and tie a knot.

4 Place the needle at the base of the nose and push it through to the back. Bring the needle through to the front and out just above the nose. Thread a bead onto the needle, place the needle right next to where it just came out and push it through to the back. This makes an eye. Repeat the above step to make the other eye. Push the needle through to the front once more to the spot where you want the mouth. Place the needle right next to where it is coming out of the head and push it through to the back. Push the needle through to the back and tie off the thread and clip the ends. Glue small bits of brown fiber to the head to make hair. Glue the green ribbon around the top hat. Glue the hat to the head. Brush on a little powdered blush to make cheeks.

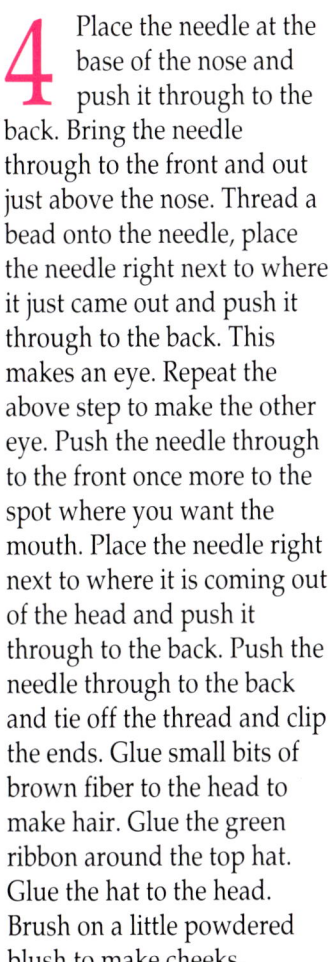

5 Fold and glue the green felt into thirds to make the sleeves.

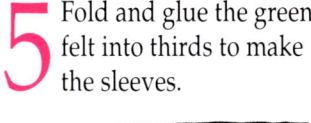

6 Cut out the hands from the pink felt and glue them into the sleeves.

7 Using a serrated steak knife, trim off 1" from one end of the styrofoam ball to make the top of the pot and 1/2" from the other end to make bottom of the pot. Press down with your fingers into the top of the pot to make a mound for the gold. Paint the styrofoam black. Use acrylics whenever you paint styrofoam. It will not dissolve the foam like enamel paints will. Glue the glitter onto the mound in the pot. Stick the ends of the chenille stem into the pot to make the handle. Glue the leprechaun so his arms are wrapped around the pot of gold.

LEVEL: 3
TIME: 60 min.
COST: $ 1

NO-BAKE GINGERBREAD HOUSE

Materials:
- graham crackers (walls and roof)
- wafer cookies (shutters)
- 1 ea. empty quart milk carton
- 17 red hots
- 11 Lifesavers
- 4 candy canes
- 5 teddy bear crackers
- 2 peppermints
- #3 and #18 cake decorating tips
- 1 ea. coupler
- 1 ea. 10" cake decorating bag
- serrated steak knife
- 1 batch of royal icing

royal icing:
- 3 med. egg whites, room temp.
- 1/2 tsp. cream of tartar
- 1 lb. powdered sugar

1 To make royal icing mix the ingredients together at high speed for 10 minutes in a grease-free bowl, preferably glass or metal. The bowl, tips and bag must be grease-free or the icing won't hold it's shape or set up properly. Keep the bowl of icing covered with a damp cloth to keep it from drying up.

2 Wash out the milk carton. Close the carton and staple it shut. Using a graham cracker as a guide, measure the carton and trim off excess from the bottom.

3 Spread a layer of icing on one side of the carton and press a graham cracker into it. Repeat for the other three sides. Trim two graham crackers with the serrated knife to form triangular pieces to go under the eaves of the roof. Attach them with icing . Attach graham crackers to the top of the carton with more icing to create the roof.

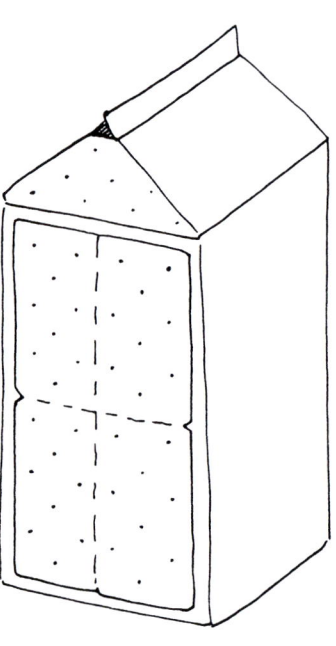

4 Place the larger piece of the coupler down into the decorating bag. Place the coupler nut around the #18 decorating tip and attach it to the bag. Fill the bag half full with icing and fold the top of the bag down.

5 Slide the tip of a knife down inside the wafer cookies to open them. Scrape off the cookie filling to make the cookies stick better to the walls of the house. Trim the cookies with a knife to make shutters. Attach the wafer cookies to the house with icing to make a door and shutters for the windows.

6 Corners of the house: with the #18 tip, fill up the space between the graham crackers in the corners with a zigzag line of icing. With the knife, trim off the curved end of a candy cane and press the remaining straight piece into the same zigzag line of icing. Repeat for the other three corners.

7 Attach the lifesavers all around the base of the house. Attach a teddy bear cracker on each side of the door and one to each side of the house just above the lifesavers.

8 With the #18 tip, squeeze out a line of icing all around the edge of the roof. Make a zigzag of icing along the top edge of the roof and press a line of 16 red hots into the icing. Change the tip to #3 and make windows in between the shutters. Attach a red hot to the door to make a door knob.

9 Attach the peppermints under the eaves on each side of the house. Squeeze out lines of icing hanging from the roof with the #3 tip to form icicles.

Use the above decorating instructions to get started and have fun creating your own ideas with other kinds of candies and cookies. These ingredients are all edible and will last one holiday season. It is just about impossible to overdo it when decorating your house so have fun piling on the goodies!

LEVEL: 3
TIME: 60 min.
COST: approx. $3.00

MOLDED CHOCOLATE CANDY

Materials:
- molding chocolate
- plastic candy mold
- paint brush
- clean jar
- small sauce pan

fondant filling:
- 1/3 cup margarine
- 1/3 cup lt. corn syrup
- 1 lb. powdered sugar
- flavoring (concentrated fruit juice, powdered drink mix, candy oil, etc. flavor to taste)

1. Mix the ingredients together and knead it by hand for a few minutes. Store in an air tight container in the refrigerator.

2. Place some pieces of molding chocolate in a clean, dry jar. Place the jar in a sauce pan that has 1" of water in it. Melt the chocolate on the stove on low heat. Do not overheat the candy or add water to it or it will get lumpy.

3. Fill the mold cavities 1/3 full with the melted chocolate. Using the paint brush, spread the chocolate around until the cavity is evenly coated. Place the mold in the refrigerator for a few minutes until the chocolate hardens.

4. Fill each cavity with some fondant.

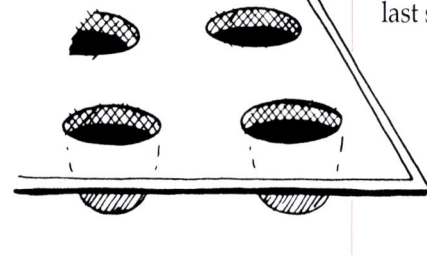

5. Spoon more chocolate into the mold to seal it. Place the mold back in the refrigerator for a few minutes.

6. Invert the mold over a towel for padding and tap gently. If the candy does not drop out of the mold, place it back into the refrigerator for a few more minutes and repeat the last step.

7. Do not freeze the candy. Excess chocolate will keep up to six months in an air tight container in the cupboard. If the candy is too old it will be lumpy when you try to melt it, and it may taste stale.

8. You can mix in raisins, peanuts, crispy rice cereal, marshmallows, coconut, small broken pieces of cookies or whatever you think sounds tasty into the melted chocolate and drop by spoonfuls onto wax paper. You can also dip pretzels, graham crackers or strawberries into the chocolate. Refrigerate for a few minutes until the candy hardens.

LEVEL: 2
TIME: 60 min.
COST: approx. $.15

PLASTER CASTING WITH MOLDS

Materials:
- plaster of paris
- plaster or candy molds
- paper clip or 18 g. wire (hanger)
- flexible plastic bowl
- disposable wooden paint stirrer
- fine sand paper
- acrylic paints
- clear acrylic spray gloss

1 Plaster casting must be done in two sessions, mixing and casting in one and painting in the other. Fill the mold with water to first determine how much will be needed for the project. Pour the water into the plastic bowl. Dry the mold off and have it ready to pour plaster into.

2 Slowly pour the plaster into the bowl. Continue pouring the plaster into the bowl until it forms a mound above the water.

3 Stir the plaster thoroughly. It will begin to thicken.

4 When it becomes a little thicker than house paint, pour it into the mold. Gently tap the mold on a hard surface to release any air bubbles trapped in the plaster.

5 Give the plaster a couple of minutes to start to set up and then stick a paper clip or a small piece of wire bent into a "u" part of the way into the plaster to create a hanger.

6 Allow the plaster to set up completely before removing the cast from the mold. The plaster should not feel cold and damp. Thin parts of the cast may break if you try to remove it too soon. After removing the cast from the mold, smooth any rough edges of the cast with sand paper.

7 To clean the plaster out of the bowl when you are finished, just press in on the sides of the bowl and the plaster will flake off. Discard any excess plaster in the trash, **NOT** down the sink. **It will clog your pipes and you will have to have it professionally removed.**

8 Paint the cast with your paints. You can make the paints dry faster by aiming a hair dryer set on low heat at them. Spray the project with acrylic gloss to seal and protect it.

LEVEL: 1
TIME: 2 sessions, 30 min. ea.
COST: approx. $.45

DOUGH ART

Materials:
1 cup all purpose flour
1/2 cup salt
1/2 cup water
paste food colors,
 acrylic or tempera paints
clear acrylic gloss spray
paper clip or 18 g. wire (hanger)
foil covered cookie sheet

1 Mix the flour, salt and water together. Knead the mixture together for ten minutes just as you would knead bread dough. This will eliminate air pockets in the dough that may expand in the oven and ruin your sculpture. To color the dough, you can mix in paste food coloring and sculpt with colored dough or paint the dough after baking. These are decorative ornaments and are not to be eaten.

2 One way to make dough art is to roll out the dough with a rolling pin and cut out shapes with a cookie cutter.

3 Another way is to sculpt the pieces by hand. It is easiest to sculpt by hand if you break down the project into basic geometric shapes such as circles, triangles, cylinders etc.

4 When sticking pieces of dough together, put a little water where the pieces will be touching each other. This will keep them together after baking.

5 Use a toothpick to make details in the dough like eyes, noses and mouths. To make the wall pocket, place a couple of pieces of rolled up foil in the pocket to hold its shape while it is baking.

6 To make a hanger, push a paper clip or a small piece of wire bent into the shape of a "u" into the back of the projects before baking.

7 When baking thin items, bake at 325° for 30 minutes on a foil covered cookie sheet and watch for burning. When baking thick items, bake at 250° for 2-4 hours or longer if needed. If a brown "cookie" look is desired, turn the temperature up to 325° for the last half hour.

8 Paint cooled dough with acrylic or tempera paint if desired and give the finished piece a couple coats of spray gloss to protect it.

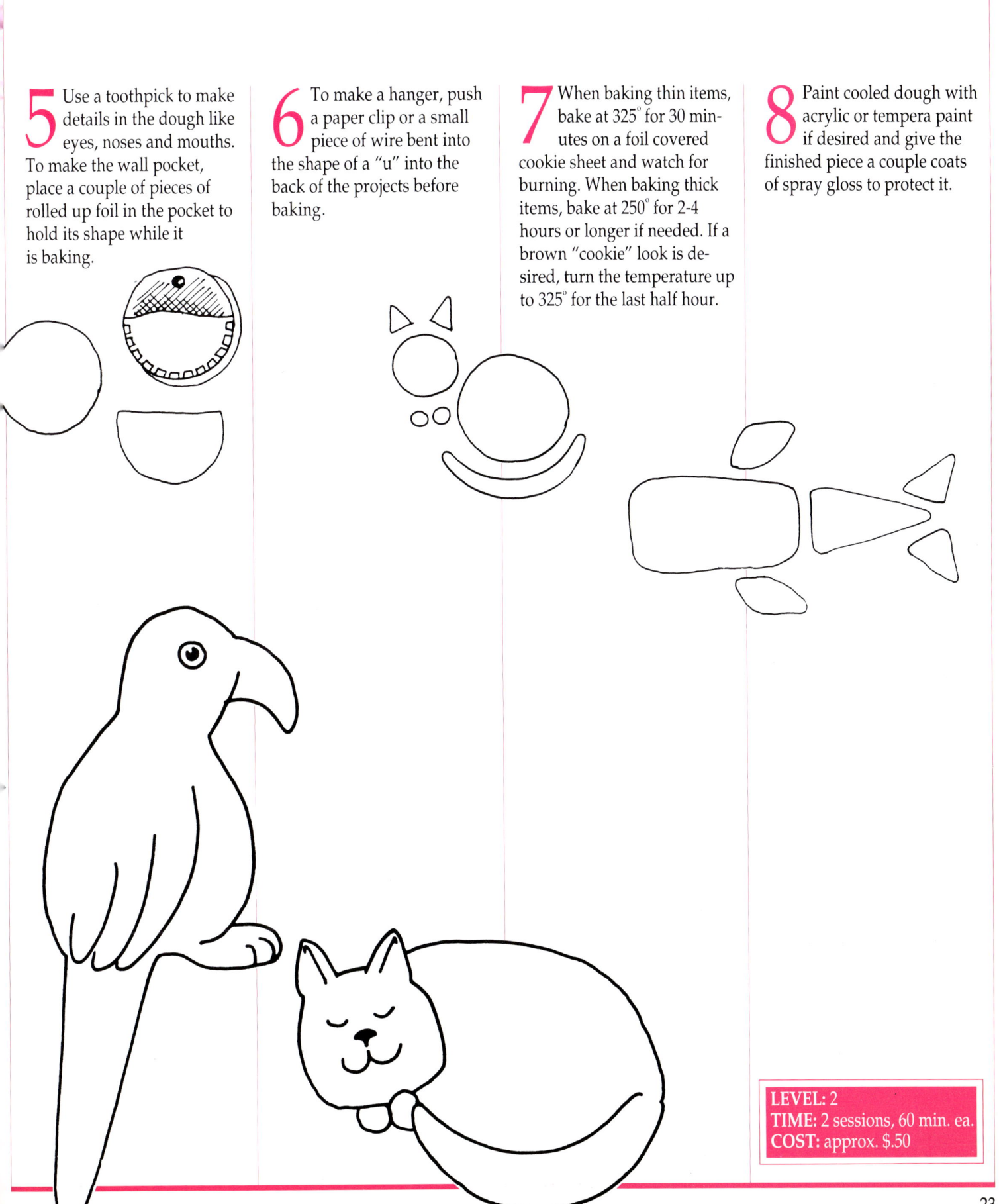

LEVEL: 2
TIME: 2 sessions, 60 min. ea.
COST: approx. $.50

MAGICIAN'S HELPER

Materials:
- 1 ea. 45 mm black plastic top hat
- 1 ea. 1" white pom pom (head)
- 1 ea. 1 1/2" white pom pom (body)
- 3 ea. 1/4" white pom poms (cheeks and tail)
- 4 ea. 1/2" white pom poms (feet)
- 1 ea. 3 mm pink pom pom (nose)
- 2 ea. 3 mm half round beads (eyes)
- 2" sq. of white felt (ears)
- tacky craft glue

1 Glue the 1" pom pom to the 1 1/2" pom pom to make the head and body.

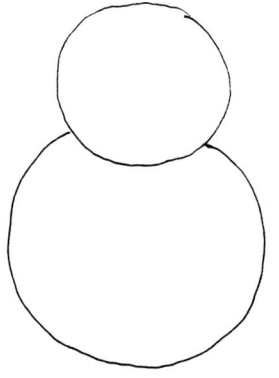

2 Cut out the ears from the felt and glue them to the head.

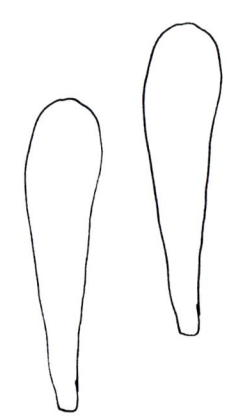

3 Glue the 1/4" pom poms to the head to make the cheeks. Glue the 3 mm pom pom just above the cheeks to make the nose. Glue the half round beads to the head to make the eyes. Glue the 1/2" pom poms to the body to make the feet and the last 1/4" pom pom to the bunny's backside to make the tail.

4 Push the bunny down into the hat.

LEVEL: 2
TIME: 20 min.
COST: approx. $.75

BAT PENCIL

Materials:
1 ea. 3/4" black pom pom (head)
1 ea. 1" black pom pom (body)
2" x 3" piece of black felt (wings and ears)
2 ea. 5 mm movable eyes
pencil
tacky craft glue

1 Glue the 3/4" pom pom to the 1" pom pom to make the bat's head and body.

2 Cut out the wings from the felt and glue them to the back of the bat.

3 Cut out the ears from the felt and glue them to the top of the bat's head. Glue the eyes to the bat's head.

4 Glue the bat onto the end of the pencil.

A simple, easy Halloween project that will delight kids of all ages. Perfect for the stay-at-home trick-or-treater!

LEVEL: 2
TIME: 20 min.
COST: approx. $.30

HOLIDAY BEAR PIN

Materials:
1 ea. 1 1/2" tan pom pom (head)
2 ea. 3/4" tan pom poms (paws)
3 ea. 1/2" tan pom poms (ears and snout)
3 ea. 3 mm half round beads (eyes and nose)
6" green garland stem (wreath)
3 ea. 5 mm red pom poms (holly berries)
1" pin-back
small pieces of plastic holly
tacky craft glue

1. Glue the 1/2" pom poms to the 1 1/2" pom pom to make the bear's ears and snout. Glue the 3/4" pom poms just underneath the bear's chin to make the two paws.

2. Bend the green garland stem into a circle and twist the ends together to form a wreath. Glue the wreath to the paws.

3. Glue the 1" pin-back to the back of the bear's head.

4. Glue small pieces of holly to the wreath and the 5 mm red pom poms to the center of the holly.

LEVEL: 1
TIME: 20 min.
COST: approx. $.65

CHOCOLATE SODA MAGNET

Materials:
1 ea. 1" white pom pom (whipped cream)
1 ea. 1" brown pom pom (or color to match the soda flavor)
1 ea. 1/4" red pom pom (cherry)
1 ea. 1 1/4" tall clear plastic cup
2" length of small straw
1" length of magnetic strip
tacky craft glue

1 Glue the magnetic strip to the side of the cup. To make the magnetic strip hold better to the cup, sand the spot on the plastic cup where you will glue the magnetic strip.

2 Glue the brown pom pom into the plastic cup. Glue the white pom pom on top of the brown pom pom. Glue the red pom pom on top of the white pom pom. Glue the straw down into the cup.

Kids love these magnets, especially on the refrigerator door where they can display very special artwork!

LEVEL: 1
TIME: 10 min.
COST: approx. $.25

SKELETON

Materials:
- 1 ea. 1 1/2" white pom pom (head)
- 1 ea. 1" white pom pom (jaw)
- 8 ea. 3/4" white pom poms (joints)
- 4 ea. 12" white chenille stems (bones)
- 1 1/2" sq. piece of black felt (features)
- extra thick tacky craft glue or low heat glue gun

1 Glue the 1 1/2" pom pom to the 1" pom pom to make the skeleton's head and jaw.

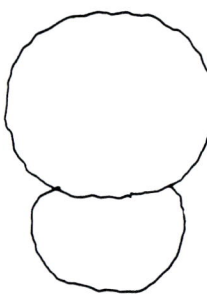

2 Cut out the eyes, nose, and mouth from the felt and glue them to the head. For a fast and easy way to cut out the mouth, use pinking shears.

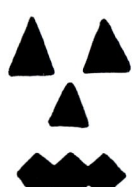

3 Cut and bend the chenille stems into pieces that match the skeleton's bones in the diagram. Glue the bones to each other and to the 3/4" pom poms to create the shoulders, elbows, hips, and knees.

4 Glue the head to the neck. Bend the ends of the arms and the legs to form hands and feet.

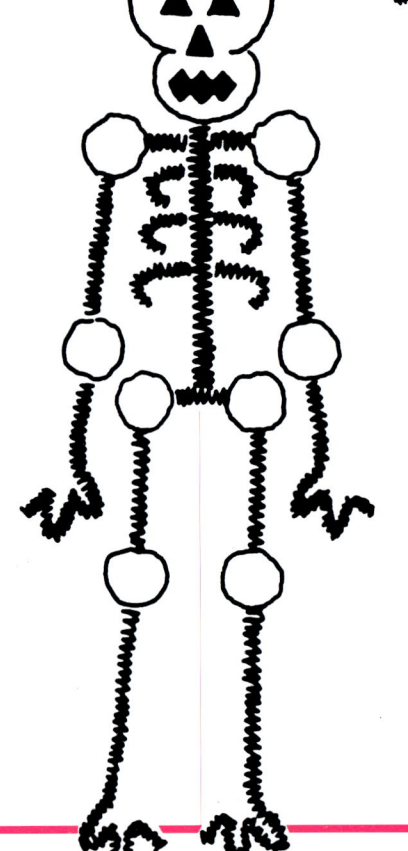

Having a party this Halloween? How about some spooky party favors hanging in the hall and doorways? Or maybe a string of them in the window.

LEVEL: 2
TIME: 30 min.
COST: approx. $.75

CANDY CANE REINDEER

Materials:
1 ea. 7" candy cane
2 ea. 7 mm movable eyes
1 ea. 12" brown chenille stem
1 ea. 5 mm red pom pom
tacky craft glue

1 Leave the cellophane wrapping on the candy cane. Cut the chenille stem in half. Twist one of the pieces around the curved end of the candy cane to make the antlers.

2 Cut the other half of the stem into two pieces 2" long and two pieces 1" long. Twist a 1" and a 2" piece around each side of the antlers.

3 Glue the eyes onto the candy cane. Glue the red pom pom to the candy cane to make the nose. You can use a different size of candy cane but you will want to change the size of the eyes and nose to fit it.

4 When working with very young children, don't cut the chenille stem up. Just attach the whole stem at its midpoint to the candy cane and bend each side of the stem into a zigzag to form the antlers.

Not only do these candy canes make great ornaments and stocking stuffers, but they're decorated on the outside of the wrapper, making them completely edible!

LEVEL: 1
TIME: 10 min.
COST: approx. $.35

CHENILLE STEM PEOPLE

Materials:
1 ea. 1" pom pom

2 ea. 12" chenille stems, one each of two colors

1 Place the pom pom in the middle of one of the chenille stems. Wrap the stem around the pom pom and twist the two ends of the stem together right next to the pom pom. Continue to twist the two ends together for about 2". The two ends of the stem are the legs.

2 Place the middle of the second chenille stem at the point where you stopped twisting the first stem and wrap it around the first stem a couple of times.

3 Wrap one end around and up the first stem creating an arm. Repeat for the other end of the stem to make the other arm.

4 Bend the arms and legs to pose your chenille person. Make shoulders, elbows, wrists, knees and ankles.

LEVEL: 1
TIME: 5 min.
COST: $ .15

BUTTERFLY NECKLACE

Materials:
- 3 ea. 1/2" black pom poms (body)
- 4" x 4" piece of orange felt (wings)
- 6" black chenille stem (antennae)
- 2 ea. 3 mm movable eyes
- 24" length of 1/8" orange satin ribbon
- tacky craft glue

1. Cut out the wings from the felt.

2. Lay the orange satin ribbon along the middle of one of the wings.

3. Fold this wing over and pinch it up in the center. Pinch the second wing up in the center and place it just under the first wing.

4. Wrap the chenille stem around the two wings and bend the ends to form the antennae.

5. Glue the three pom poms together to form the butterfly's body. Glue the body to the center of the wings. Glue the eyes to the head. Tie the ends of the satin ribbon together to make the necklace.

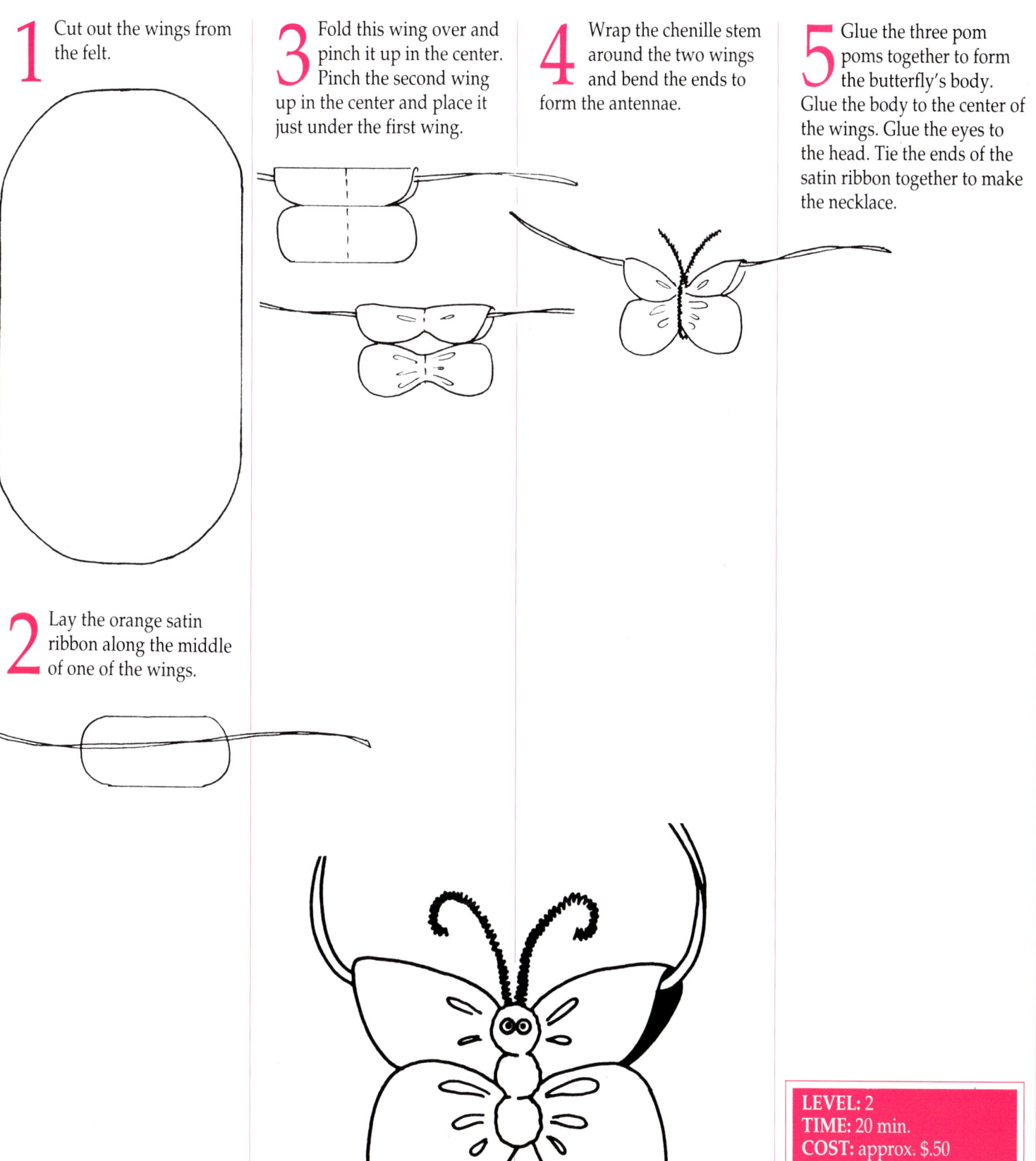

LEVEL: 2
TIME: 20 min.
COST: approx. $.50

FOAM CRITTER- SNAIL MAGNET

Materials:
- foam packing chip, S-shaped
- 1 ea. 3" bump chenille
- 2 ea. 5 mm movable eyes
- 1 ea. flower stamen (antennae)
- small piece of magnetic strip
- tacky craft glue

1 Bend the bump chenille around one end of the chip to form the fuzzy body of your snail. Stick the ends of the bump chenille down into the chip and glue them in place, being careful not to break the chip.

2 Glue two eyes to the other end of the chip to form the head.

3 Glue a piece of magnetic strip to one side of the foam chip. The snail is fragile so handle it gently.

4 Cut the flower stamen in half to form two 1/2" antennae. Poke two holes into the head with a pin and glue the antennae into the holes.

These cute little guys are so fast and easy to make, you'll be busy making them by the hundreds! A family of four or five make a terrific gift!

LEVEL: 1
TIME: 20 min.
COST: approx. $.20

BUMP CHENILLE HEART

Materials:
1 ea. red 2-bump chenille	1 ea. red chenille stem

1 Bend and twist the 2-bump chenille into a heart. Twist the ends together.

2 Slide the chenille stem halfway through the middle of the heart and twist the two ends tightly together to form a stem.

You can give someone more than just a card for Valentine's day... how about making that special someone a gift like this? What a sweetheart.

LEVEL: 1
TIME: 5 min.
COST: $ .15

BUMP CHENILLE SHAMROCKS

Materials:
15 ea. green bump chenille
2 ea. green chenille stems

1 Cut a length of six bumps from the 15 bump chenille. With this length bend and twist two bumps into a heart. Bend and twist the next two bumps together to make another heart. Bend and twist the last two bumps together to form the third heart. Bend and twist these three hearts together to form a shamrock.

2 Make a second shamrock with six more bumps.

3 With the remaining bumps make three simple loops to form a bud.

4 Slide an end of one of the chenille stems over and through the middle heart in one of the shamrocks. Fold it down about 2" from the end and twist it tightly to itself. This makes a 10" stem for this shamrock. Cut the other stem in half and repeat the above step with these two pieces and the other shamrock and bud. Attach the three shamrocks together.

Ever wonder how to dress up a St. Patrick's day party table? Add some shamrocks to each place setting, or maybe tuck them into a floral centerpiece!

LEVEL: 1
TIME: 20 min.
COST: $ .75

REMOTE CONTROL HOLDER

Materials:
12 ea. jumbo craft sticks
acrylic paint, two colors
6 ea. craft sticks
extra thick tacky craft glue or low heat glue gun

1 Glue three jumbo craft sticks together to form one side of the holder. Glue three more jumbo craft sticks together to form the other side. Let the glue dry completely before moving on to the next step.

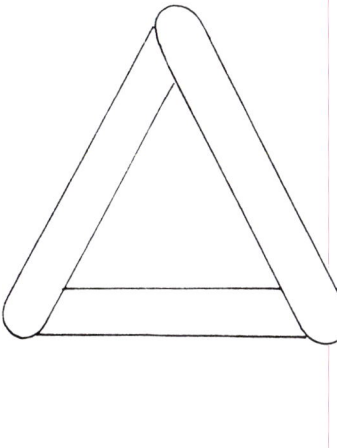

2 Have another person help hold the sides up while you do the next step. Glue two regular craft sticks inside each of the three corners to hold the sides up. If using craft glue, you will have to prop up the two sides while the craft sticks in the corners are drying.

3 Glue three jumbo craft sticks across the front of the holder and three more across the back side of the holder. When the glue is dry, paint the holder.

4 Paint a special message across the front of the holder like "My Dad (or Mom, Brother, Sister, etc.) is a remote control maniac".

LEVEL: 2
TIME: 1 session, 60 min. if using glue gun. 4 sessions, 10 min. each if using craft glue.
COST: approx. $.85

JAIL BANK

Materials:
85 craft sticks
brown, gold and black acrylic paint
extra thick tacky craft glue or low heat gun

1. Lay out twelve craft sticks. Glue one stick across the top edge and one across the bottom edge of these sticks. This will make the bottom of the bank. Repeat this step four more times to make the four sides of the bank. Let the glue dry before going to the next step.

2. Glue the four sides and the bottom together. If using craft glue, you will have to prop up the four walls while they are drying.

3. When the glue is completely dry, glue eleven sticks across the top of the bank leaving a space open near the middle. This space is the coin slot. Glue two sticks up on their sides along the coin slot to make the slot narrow. Let the glue dry.

4. Paint the bank brown, the door black, the windows gold and the bars on the windows and the door black. Paint a black rectangle above the door. Paint **$ JAIL $** with gold paint in this rectangle.

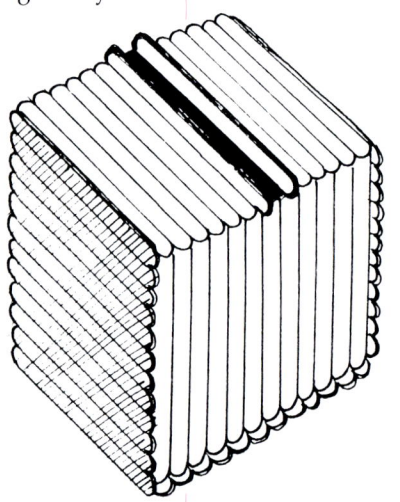

LEVEL: 2
TIME: 60 min. if using glue gun
4 sessions, 20 min. each if using craft glue.
COST: approx. $1.25

HORSE

Materials:
five flat clothespins
one craft stick (ears)
one jumbo craft stick (saddle)
9" pieces of 1/4" jute (rope-like fiber—for the mane and tail)
acrylic paints—black, white, brown and dark brown
waterbase varnish
extra thick tacky craft glue

1 Cut three clothespins along Line #1. Take one of the thin pieces and cut it along line #2 to make a 2" long piece for the neck.

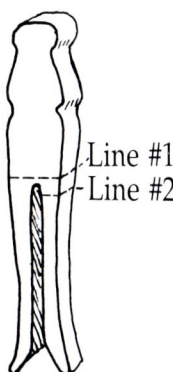

2 Glue two of the cut clothespins between the two uncut clothespins to form the body and legs.

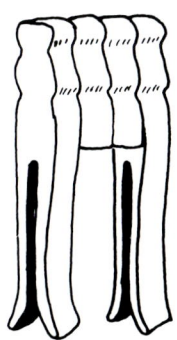

3 Glue the 2" piece to the body to create the neck. Glue the third cut clothespin to the neck to form the head.

4 Cut 1/2" from one end of the craft stick, split this 1/2" piece lengthwise into two pieces and glue them to the head to make the ears.

5 Cut a 1" piece from both ends of the jumbo craft stick, cut a 3/4" piece from this same stick. Glue these pieces to the horse to create the saddle. Let glue dry completely before moving on to next step.

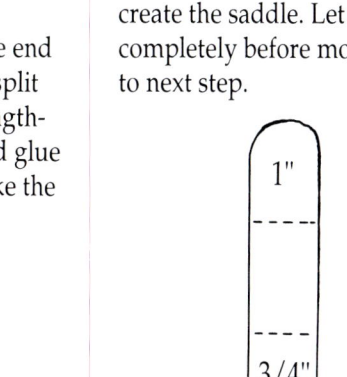

6 Paint the horse brown and the saddle dark brown. Paint the eyes, hooves, and nostrils black. Paint tiny white dots for reflection in the eyes. Let paint dry and varnish.

7 Cut a 3" length of jute and glue it to the horse's backside to make the tail. Cut the remaining jute into 1" pieces and glue them to the head and neck to make the mane. Fray the jute on the mane and tail and trim with scissors.

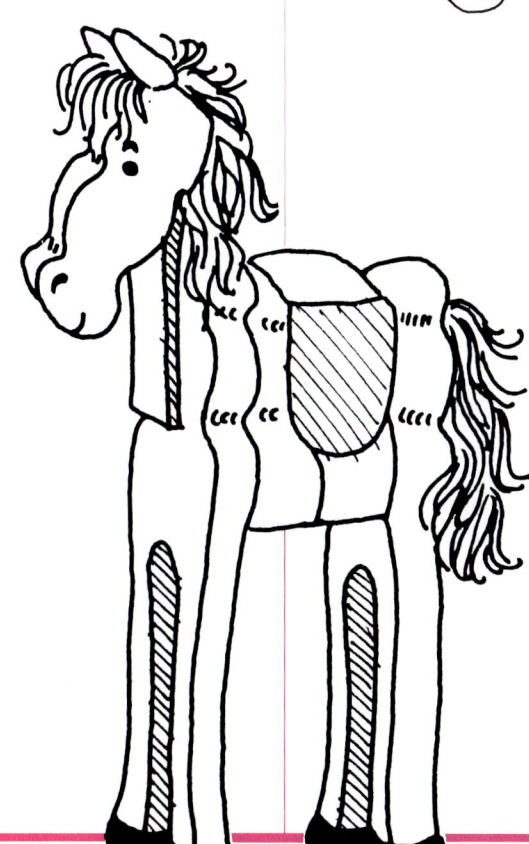

LEVEL: 3
TIME: 2 sessions. 60 min. ea.
COST: $1.75

MOUSE 'N CHEESE

Materials:
one round clothespin
1 1/2" square of gray felt (ear)
1" square of pink felt (inner ear)
2 1/2" piece of gray chenille stem (tail)
two 1/4" gray pom poms (paws)
2" square of 1" thick styrofoam (cheese)
8" length of metalic thread (hanger)
acrylic paint—gray, black, pink and orange
waterbase varnish
extra thick tacky craft glue

1 Cut the ears from the gray and pink felt. Glue the pink inner ears to the gray ears.

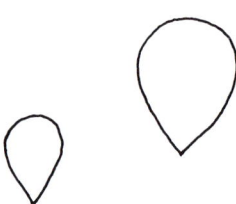

2 Cut the clothespin as shown to create the mouse's head and body. Paint the eyes and whiskers black and the nose pink. Let the paint dry and varnish.

3 Sand the paint away from the back of the head where the ears belong. Glue the ears to this spot.

4 Glue the pom poms to the body to form the paws.

5 Cut the foam into a triangle to make the cheese as shown below. Paint the cheese orange.

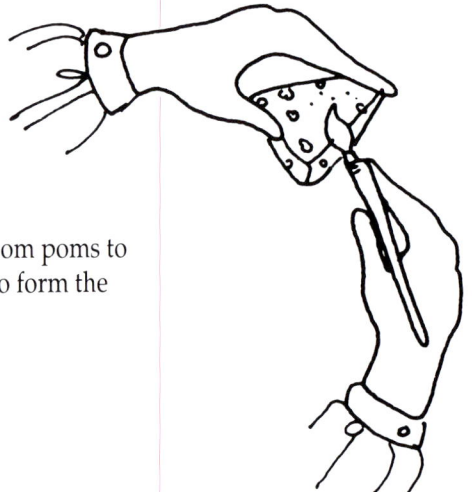

6 Press the mouse down into the cheese to make a hole. Glue the mouse in place in the hole. Glue the chenille stem into the backside of the cheese to form the mouse's tail.

7 Tie the metallic thread into a loop and attach it to the mouse to form a hanger.

LEVEL: 2
TIME: 60 min.
COST: $.75

PENCIL HOLDER

Materials:
twenty-four craft sticks
one 1lb. can with the label removed
acrylic paints—blue and white
extra thick tacky craft glue or
low heat glue gun

1 Glue the craft sticks to the can. Place two rubber bands around the can to hold the sticks in place. Let glue dry completely and then remove the rubber bands.

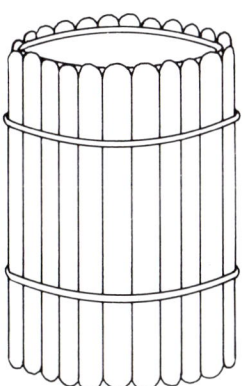

2 Paint the craft sticks blue.

3 Transfer the design of your choice onto the craft sticks. Paint the design white with blue stitching. Let dry and varnish.

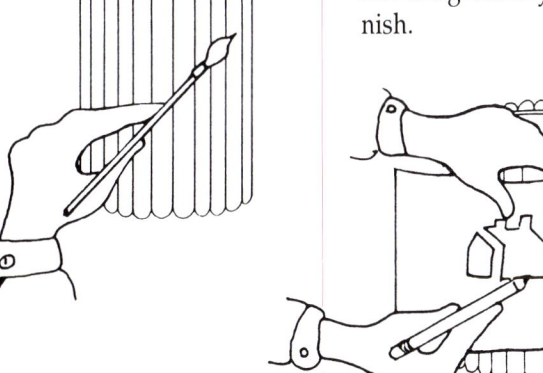

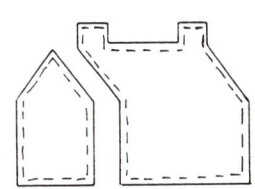

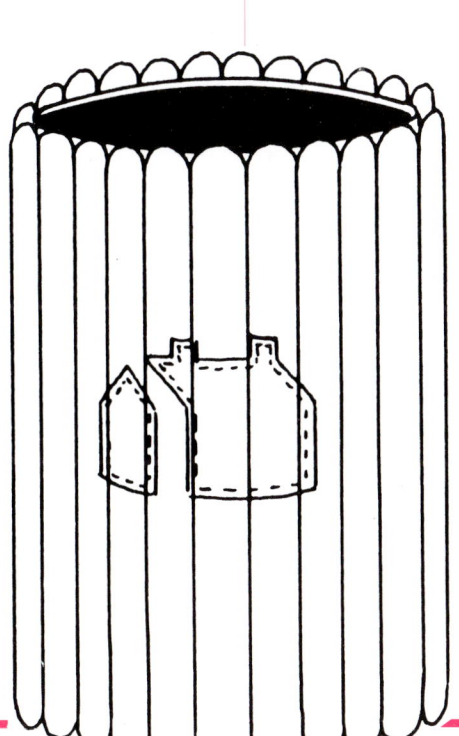

LEVEL: 1
TIME: 2 sessions, 20 min. ea.
COST: $1.25

DECORATIVE PAINTING ON CUT-OUTS

Materials:
small wooden cut-outs (available at most craft stores)
acrylic paints, assorted colors
water based varnish
round toothpick
fine sandpaper or an emery board
1 ea. sheet of tracing paper
paper towels
old plate

1 This first step will keep your acrylics from drying up while you are working: Place a couple layers of paper towels on top of an old plate. Pour water onto the towels until they are completely saturated. Pour off excess water and place a sheet of tracing paper on top of the wet towels. Place a little puddle of your acrylics on top of the tracing paper.

2 Sand any rough edges on the wood. If you want to hang your project from a metallic thread when it is finished, tap a hole in it with a hammer and small nail before you paint it.

3 Paint the cut-out with two or three coats of paint of the background color, letting each coat dry. You can speed up the drying time for acrylic paint by blowing warm air from a hair dryer on it.

4 Painting Techniques: Make dots by dipping the end of the toothpick into the paint and touching it to the wood. Make larger dots by dipping the handle of your paint brush into the paint and touching it to the wood. Dots made this way make great eyes for animal cut outs. Make five dots in a circle with a larger dot of a different color in the center and you have a flower. Place two dots next to each other so that they just touch. Pull down and inward with each dot and you have a small heart. Make small lines in a row with a liner brush and you have stitches. Thin the paint a little with water when making stitches. Combine stitches and dots to make interesting borders for your cut outs.

5 Brush on a coat of water based varnish. Attach the metallic thread to the cut out to make a hanger.

LEVEL: 2
TIME: 60 min.
COST: $ 2.00

DECOUPAGE CHRISTMAS PLAQUE

Materials:
1 ea. wood plaque
print of your choice (wrapping paper, postcard, greeting card, etc.)
water based decoupage medium
acrylic paints, colors of your choice
decorative hanger for the top of the project or a sawtooth hanger for the back of it

1 Paint the wood plaque the color of your choice. Paint the back of the plaque so that your project is neat.

2 While the paint is drying, cut out the print that you want to decoupage. The word decoupage comes from a french word meaning "to cut."

3 Brush a layer of decoupage medium onto the plaque. Let it dry.

4 Brush a layer of medium onto the back of the print and press it down on the plaque. Gently rub out any air bubbles or excess medium. Let dry.

5 Brush three coats of medium onto the plaque, letting each coat dry before adding another.

6 Attach the hanger to the plaque when the final coat has dried. If the humidity is high where you live your project may feel sticky for a few days. Be careful where you lay it down. It may stick to paper. You can give it a light coat of spray acrylic gloss to eliminate the stickiness.

LEVEL: 2
TIME: 5 sessions 20 min. ea.

DIAMOND DUST ORNAMENT

Materials:
1 ea. 2 1/2" styrofoam ball
1 ea. paper napkin with printed design and white background
1 ea. 4" piece of tinsel stem
1 ea. 6" length of 1/4" red satin ribbon
6" piece of light weight wire
diamond dust, non-glass type
tacky craft glue

1 Tear the design out of the paper napkin, leaving a 1/2" border of the white napkin around the design. Pull the napkin layers apart so that you are only using the top layer with the design.

2 Stick the tinsel stem 1" into the ball.

3 Thin some craft glue with water and brush a coat of thin glue onto the styrofoam ball. Place the napkin with the design on top of the glue and brush another coat of glue on top of the napkin. Brush until all the edges of the napkin are flat against the ball. Sprinkle the diamond dust lightly over the entire ball and let dry.

4 Make a quick bow with the ribbon and wire and attach it to the tinsel stem. Directions for making quick bows are given on page 8. Bend the tinsel stem into a hook. You can make styrofoam Easter eggs make using the same process. Use the non-glass type of diamond dust when working with children.

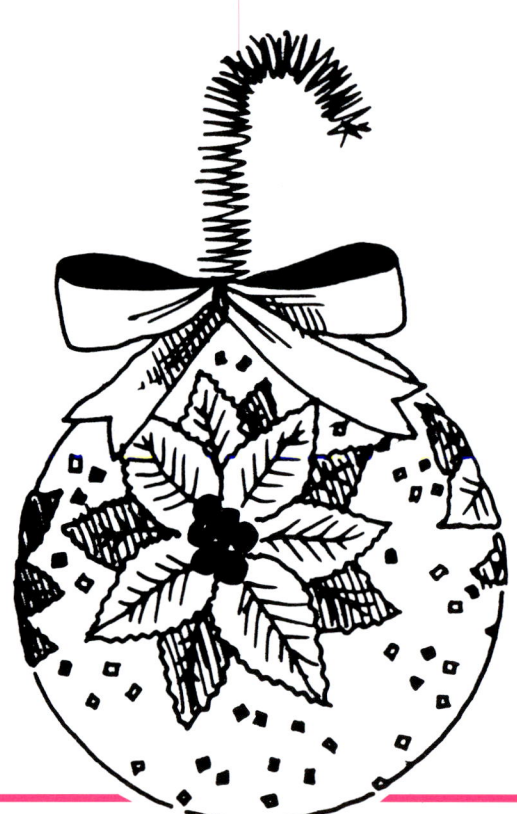

LEVEL: 1
TIME: 20 min.
COST: approx. $.75

PAPER FOLDER

Materials:
1 ea. 12"x 18" construction paper
2 ea. 10" length of 1/4" woven edge satin ribbon
#13 tapestry needle
9 1/2" length of 1 1/4" ribbon
tacky craft glue

1 Fold the paper along the dotted lines. The folds along the sides and bottom should be 2 1/2" from the edges. Trim the upper corners to make them round. Open the paper. Mark position for ribbon holes 4 1/2" from top.

2 Tie a knot in one end of a piece of ribbon. Thread the ribbon onto the needle and poke the needle through the paper at one of the marks. Pull the ribbon through until the knot is at the hole. Place a medium dab of glue on the knot as well as on the paper around the hole. This will reinforce the paper and help keep the ribbon from pulling out of the hole. Repeat for the other piece of ribbon and hole.

3 Fold the paper back up and glue the lower corners in place. Glue the 9 1/2" length of ribbon down one edge of the front of the folder. You can also paint or draw a picture or write a special message on the front.

4 This folder can be used to hold stationery and envelopes, photos, recipes, etc. If you want a sturdier folder, use lightweight poster board or bristol board. To hold the folder closed, tie the ribbons in a bow.

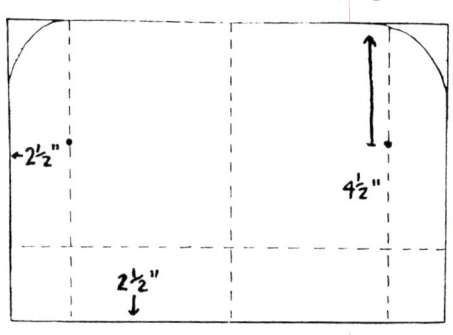

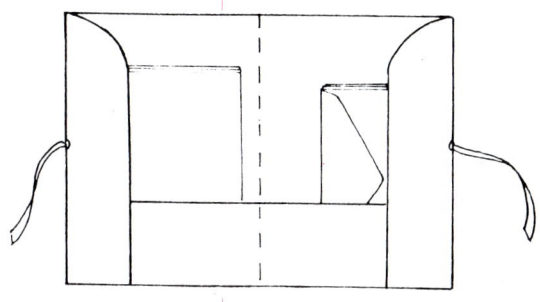

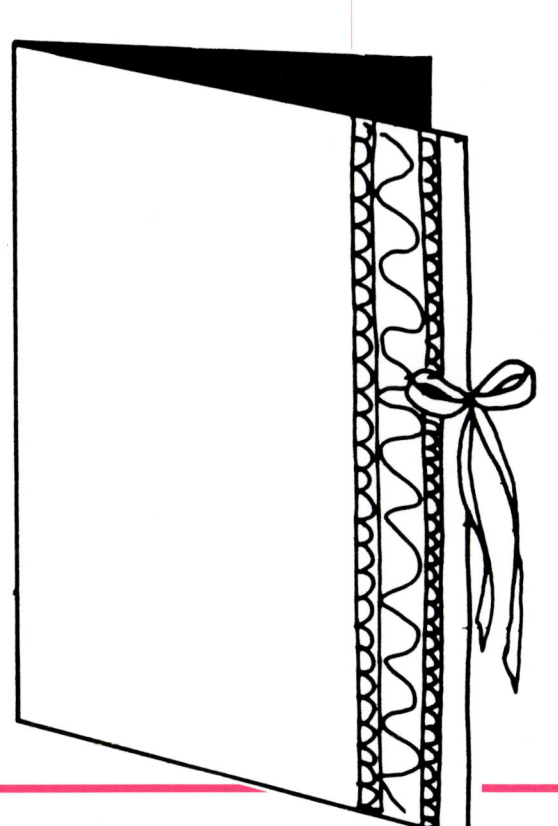

LEVEL: 1
TIME: 30 min.
COST: $ .75

BROWN BAG BASKET AND BOWS

Materials:
2 medium size brown paper bags
2 wire twist ties from bread bags

1 Trim off the top inch of one of the bags. Cut off two 1 1/2" sections from the bag.

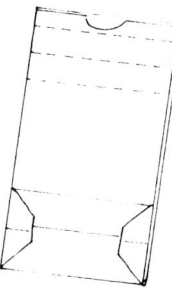

2 Clip the sections and open them up to form two strips. Trim the ends of the strips to make points.

3 Make two quick bows with the strips, wrapping the twist ties around the centers of the bows to hold them together. Directions for quick bows are given on page 8.

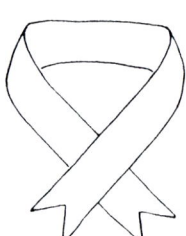

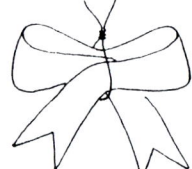

4 Take the second bag and fold down the top edge several times until the bag is the height you want.

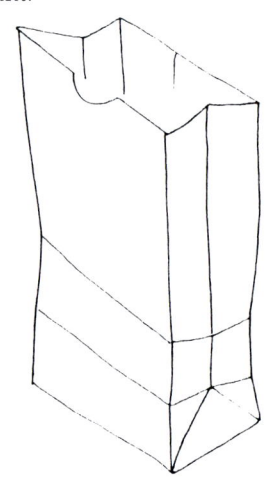

5 To attach a bow to the bag, punch two holes into the bag near the top edge and push the ends of the wire twist tie through the holes. Twist the ends together inside the bag. Attach the second bow to the opposite side of the bag in the same manner. If you use your basket to hold a small plant or food that would stain the bag (cookies, rolls, etc.), line the inside with plastic wrap. You can also stencil a design onto the bag with acrylic paints or paint the strips before you turn them into bows.

LEVEL: 1
TIME: 20 min.
COST: approx. $.15

TISSUE PAPER FLOWER

Materials:
4 ea. 7 1/2" x 10" pieces of tissue paper, 2 ea. of 2 colors
4 ea. 3 3/4" x 5" pieces of green tissue paper
2 ea. 12" green chenille stems
tacky craft glue

1 Stack the four sheets of 7 1/2" x 10" tissue paper on top of each other in any color order that you want. Fold the papers up into 1/2" accordion pleats.

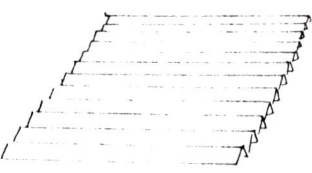

2 Wrap a chenille stem around the middle of the folded papers and twist tightly.

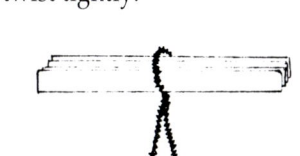

3 While the papers are still folded up, cut the ends in a curve or a point.

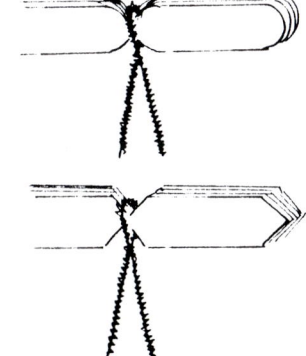

4 Gently separate the four layers of paper on both sides of the flower. If the paper should tear, just glue the torn edges back together with the tacky craft glue.

5 To make the leaf, draw the outline of the leaf onto one of the pieces of green tissue paper with tacky craft. Make vein lines and a line down the middle of the leaf with the glue. Cut the remaining chenille stem in half and press one of the pieces into the line of glue in the middle of the leaf, leaving half of the stem sticking out of the leaf. Place a second piece of green tissue paper on top of the first one and press the two pieces together. After a few minutes, cut the leaf out by trimming around the outside edge of the glue.

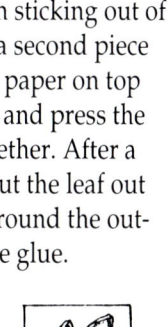

6 Make a second leaf with the remaining pieces of green tissue paper and chenille stem. Attach the leaves to the flower stem.

LEVEL: 2
TIME: 20 min.
COST: $ .25

PAPER BOX

Materials:
2 pieces of 12"x 18" construction paper
18" length of 7/8" ribbon
assorted small silk flowers
tacky craft glue

1 Trim one of the pieces of construction paper to form a 12" square. Fold the paper into a triangle.

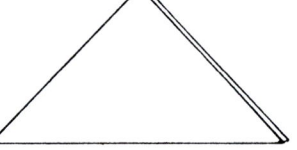

2 Open the paper.

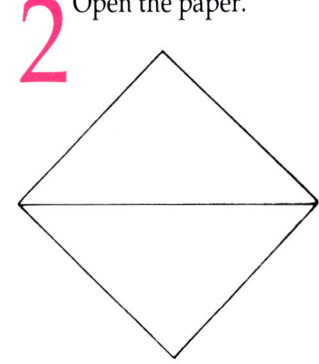

3 Fold the two corners into the middle and make new folds. Open the paper.

4 Bring the two corners up to the last folds made and make new folds. Open the paper.

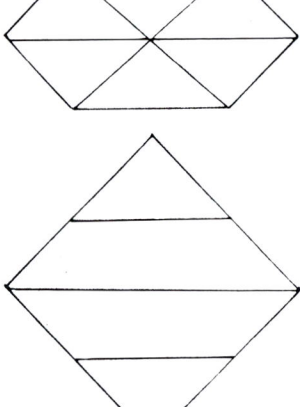

5 Bring the corners, one at a time, up to the opposite folds made and make new folds.

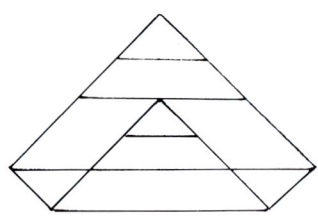

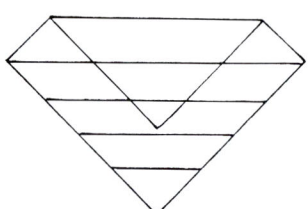

6 Turn the paper one quarter turn. Repeat the steps from 2 to 5. Your paper should be divided into twenty-four squares with sixteen triangles around the edges.

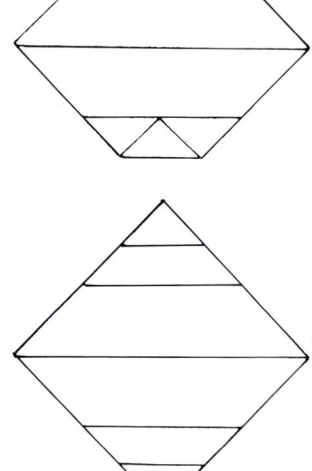

7 Cut four lines, each being two squares long.

8 Fold the two corners towards the middle, folding each one over twice. This will make two sides to the box.

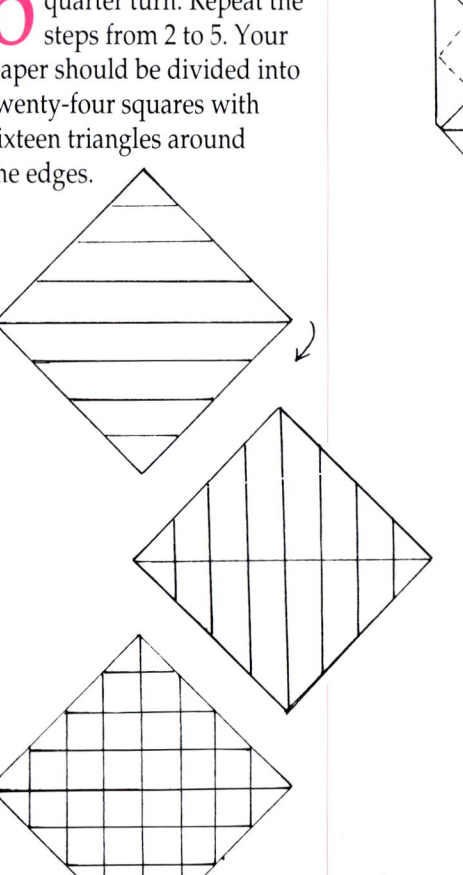

9 Bring one side up and fold the two ends in. Bring the other side up and fold its ends in.

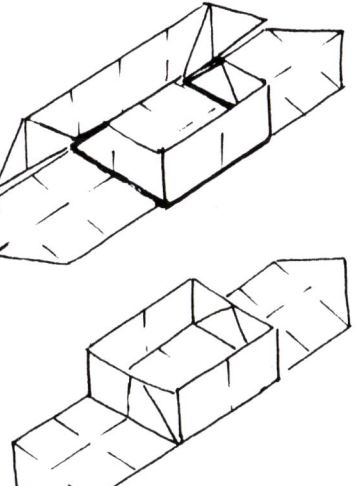

10 Bring one of the corners up, over and down into the box. Bring the other corner up, over and down into the box. Place small dots of glue under the corners to help hold the box together. You have completed one half of the box.

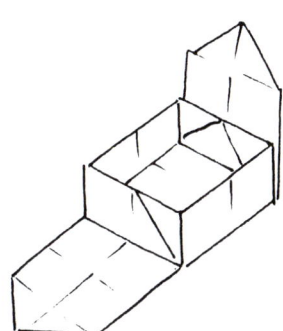

11 Repeat the entire process with the second piece of paper to make the other half of the box. One piece will fit snugly inside the other one.

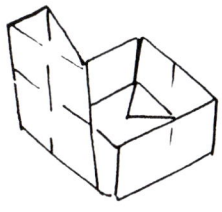
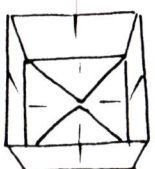

12 Glue pieces of ribbon across the top and small silk flowers to the center of the box. This paper box also makes a great container for other projects that you may want to give as gifts.

LEVEL: 2
TIME: 30 min.
COST: $ .75

PAPER BIRD

Materials:
1 ea. 8 1/2"x11" piece of paper

1 Directions: Fold the paper in half.

2 Trace the pattern onto the paper, placing the straight line of the bird's back along the fold of the paper. Cut out the bird.

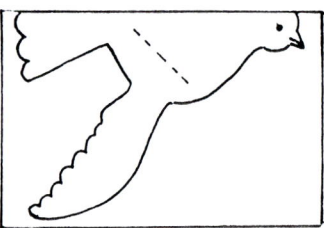

3 If you want to color or paint the bird, do so now. Cut a slit into each side of the bird.

4 Curl one wing to the inside of the bird and slide it through the slit on the same side of the bird that the wing is on. Slide the other wing through the slit on the other side of the bird. Attach a thread to the bird's back at the dot to make a hanger. Glue the edges together along the bird's forehead and beak.

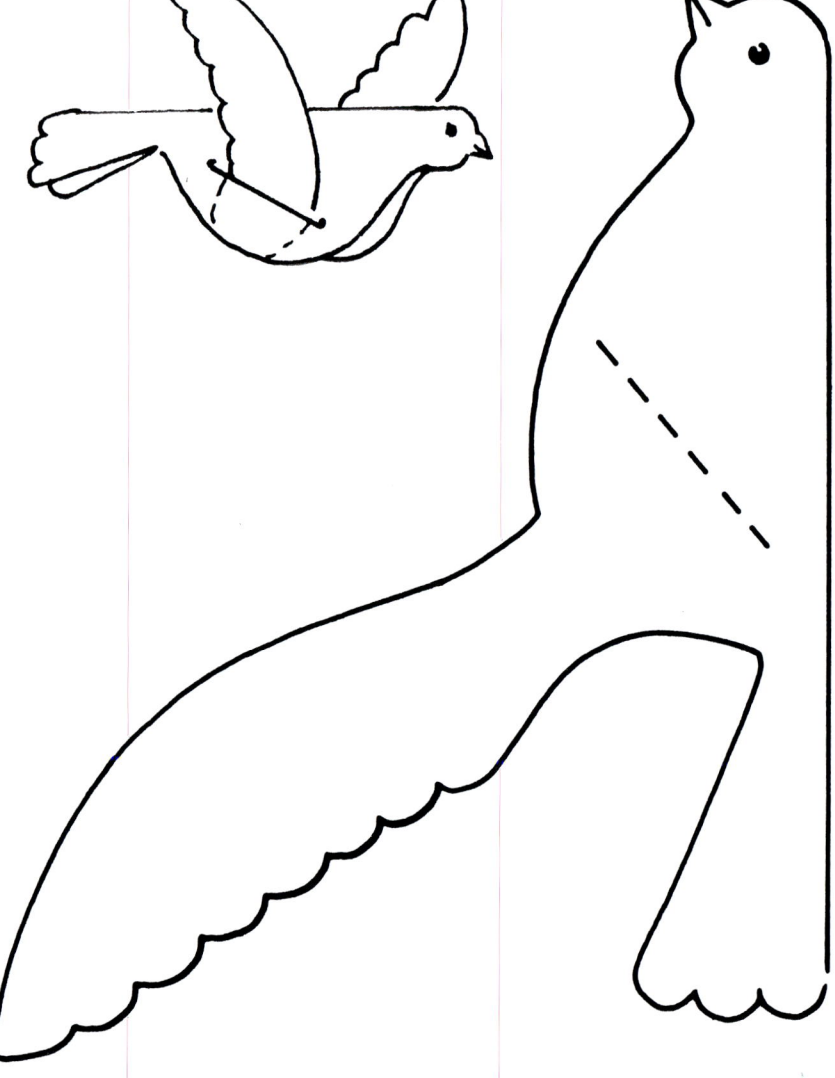

LEVEL: 1
TIME: 20 min.
COST: $ .15

PAPER ANGEL

Materials:
1 ea. 8 1/2"x11" piece of paper
colored pencils or crayons
tacky craft glue

1 Trace the pattern onto the paper and cut out the angel, halo and music sheet. To make a bigger angel, have the pattern enlarged at your local copy shop. Some papers tear easier than others. Avoid those types of paper for this project.

2 Draw the features onto the angel's face and the fingers onto the music sheet.

3 Cut slits along the dotted lines, being careful not to cut the lines too long or they will tear out.

4 To assemble, roll the angel's skirt carefully into a cone and lock the wings together at the slits. Glue the two edges of the skirt together, as well as the the wings. Place the music sheet into the slit in the angel's skirt. Place the halo on top of the angel's head. Add a dot of glue to the halo and the music sheet to hold them in place.

LEVEL: 1
TIME: 20 min.
COST: $ .15

PAPER SNOWFLAKE

Materials:
1 ea. square piece of paper the size of the snowflake you want to make

1 Trace a circle onto a piece of paper using something round that is the size of the snowflake you want to make. A bowl or plate works great. If they are not handy, use the following instructions: Fold a square piece of paper into a triangle.

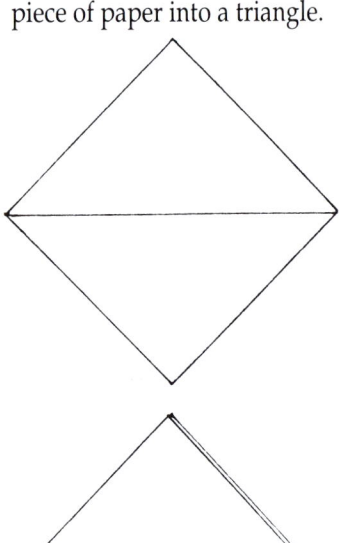

2 Bring the left corner up and over to the right and the right corner behind and up to the left to make 3 equal sections. Draw dotted line as shown.

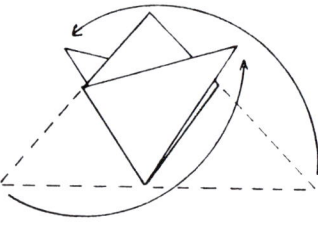

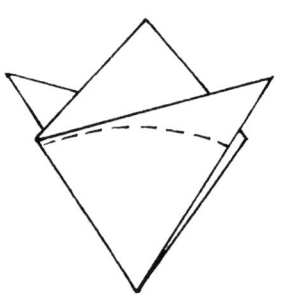

3 Cut along the dotted lines to make the circle.

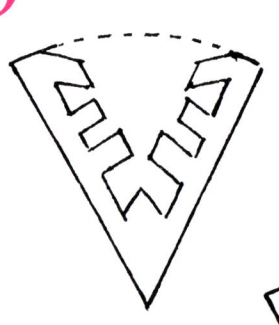

4 Keep the paper folded up. Draw your pattern onto the two edges of the paper using one of the three designs given or make up one of your own. Cut away the shaded areas and carefully open up your snowflake.

LEVEL: 1
TIME: 20 min.
COST: approx. $ .15

BEADED SNOWFLAKE

Materials:
- 1 ea. 12" white chenille stem
- 12 ea. 6 mm clear faceted beads
- 12 ea. 12 mm clear cartwheels
- 12 ea. 8 mm clear faceted beads 6 ea.
- 18 mm clear cartwheels
- 10" length of metallic thread
- tacky craft glue or a low heat glue gun

1 Cut the chenille stem into three equal pieces. Glue them together at their mid-points so that they are evenly spaced and form the six arms of a snowflake. The glue must be completely dry before continuing.

2 Thread the beads onto each of the arms in the following order: one 6 mm faceted, one 12 mm cartwheel, one 8 mm faceted, one 18 mm cartwheel, one 8 mm faceted, one 12 mm cartwheel and one 6 mm faceted bead.

3 Glue the last bead, the 6 mm faceted, in place to keep the beads from sliding off. Trim off any excess chenille stem that may be sticking out the ends.

4 Tie the metallic thread around one of the arms to form a hanger. For interesting effects, mix various colors and change the order of the beads in your snowflakes.

Snowflakes make beautiful Christmas tree ornaments! Hang them in a sunny place and see how they brighten up the room!

LEVEL: 1
TIME: 20 min. if you are using glue gun
2 sessions, 10 & 20 min. if using craft glue
COST: approx. $.50

BEADED ICICLE

Materials:
- 6" piece of silver tinsel stem
- 4 ea. 18 mm clear cartwheels
- 4 ea. 12 mm clear cartwheels
- 4 ea. 10 mm clear cartwheels
- 2 ea. 8 mm clear faceted beads
- 3 ea. 6 mm clear faceted beads
- 3 ea. 4 mm clear rondelles

1 Thread the beads onto the tinsel stem in the same order as they are given above.

2 Slide all the beads down so that the 4 mm rondelles are at one end of the tinsel stem.

3 Bend the end of the tinsel stem over to keep the beads from falling off. Bend the other end of the tinsel stem into a hook for hanging.

You'll want to make dozens of these for your tree this holiday season. Watch them sparkle next to colorful lights, creating their own magic.

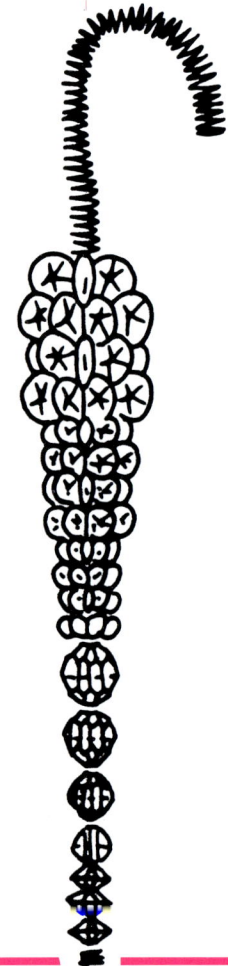

LEVEL: 1
TIME: 10 min.
COST: approx. $.25

BEADED CARTWHEEL WREATH

Materials:
1 ea. 12" red chenille stem
24 ea. 18 mm green cartwheels
12 ea. 6 mm clear faceted beads
10" length of metallic thread

1 Thread two cartwheels followed by one faceted bead onto the chenille stem. Repeat this step until all of the beads have been used up.

2 Position the beads so that the ends of the stem are the same length. Twist these ends together and bend them to form a bow.

3 Attach the metallic thread to the top of the wreath to form a hanger.

The secret to giftwrapping is in the details. For a special touch, add a tiny wreath like this one to the package... you'll be surprised at how beautiful it looks!

LEVEL: 1
TIME: 10 min.
COST: approx. $.55

BEAD AND LACE CANDY CANE

Materials:
22" length of 3/4" white insert lace
36 ea. red tri beads
6" piece of red or white chenille stem
6" length of 1/4" red satin ribbon
6" piece of light weight wire
10" length of metallic thread

1 Slide one end of the chenille stem through one of the tri beads and then through the large hole at one end of the lace. Place a second tri bead onto the stem and place the end of the stem through the next large hole in the lace. Repeat this step until all of the beads have been used, being careful to use only the large holes in the lace.

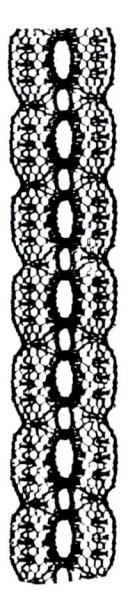

2 When all of the beads and lace have been threaded onto the stem, bend the ends over to hold the beads in place. Bend the stem into the shape of a candy cane.

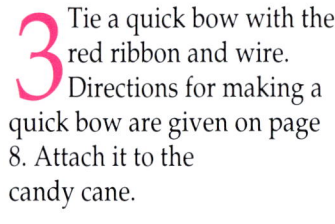

3 Tie a quick bow with the red ribbon and wire. Directions for making a quick bow are given on page 8. Attach it to the candy cane.

4 Attach the metallic thread to the top of the candy cane to form a hanger.

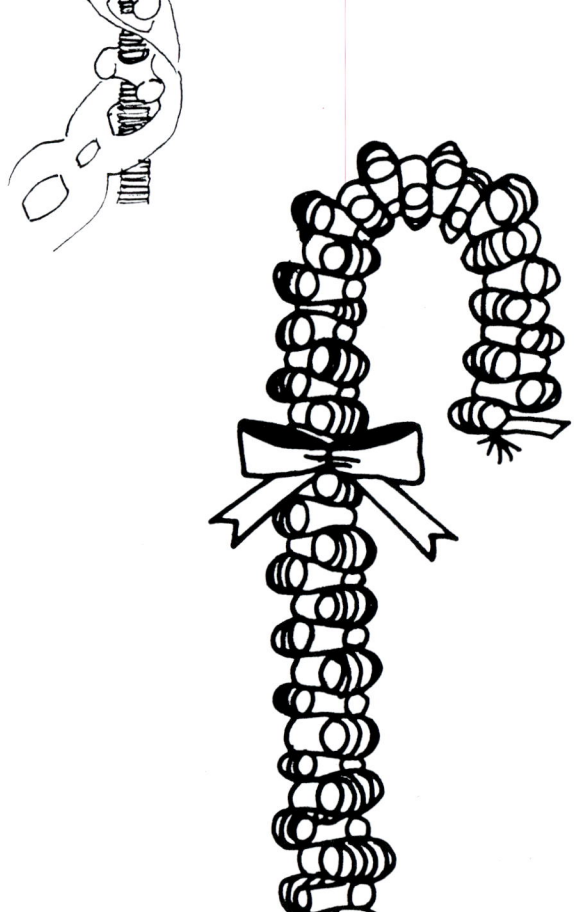

LEVEL: 2
TIME: 20 min.
COST: approx. $.50

BEAD AND LACE HEART

Materials:
32" length of 3/4" white or red insert lace
58 ea. red, clear or white tri beads
1 ea. 12" red or white chenille stem
6" length of 1/4" red satin ribbon
6" piece of light weight wire
10" length of metallic thread

1 Follow the same directions given for the Bead and Lace Candy Cane on page 54.

2 When all the tri beads have been strung onto the chenille stem, twist the ends of the stem together and trim off any excess stem. Bend the lace and beads into a heart with the ends of the stem at the bottom of the heart.

3 Tie a quick bow with the ribbon and wire and attach it to the top of the heart. Directions for making quick bows are given on page 8.

4 Tie the metallic thread onto the heart to make a hanger.

Here's another pretty Valentine project guaranteed to bring a smile to your special friend!

LEVEL: 2
TIME: 20 min.
COST: approx. $.75

BEAD AND LACE CANDLE

Materials:
7" length of 3/4" green insert lace
12 ea. clear tri beads
1 ea. 12" metallic tinsel stem
1 ea. red spaghetti bead

1 Follow the same directions for the Bead and Lace Candy Cane on page 54 for threading the tri beads onto the tinsel stem.

2 Slide on the spaghetti bead after the last tri bead, bending a little of the tinsel stem over to hold the bead on. These steps create the candle and flame.

3 Bend the remaining tinsel stem so that it forms a 1 1/2" circle around the base of the candle. This circle holds the candle up.

4 Bend and twist the end of the tinsel stem to form a handle for the candle holder. This ornament is made to sit on a table but you may attach a 10" length of metallic thread to the candle to make a hanger.

This ornament is made to sit on a table, but you can think of lots of other uses too... be creative!

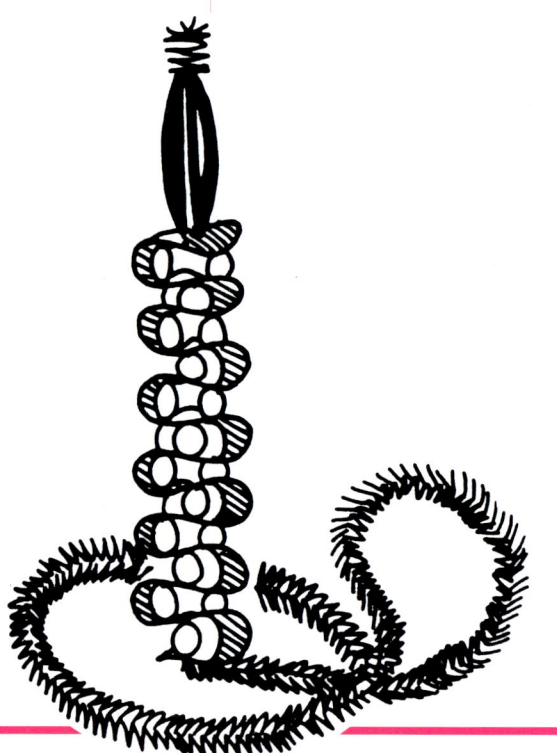

LEVEL: 2
TIME: 20 min.
COST: approx. $.35

LACE ANGEL

Materials:
20" piece of 3 1/2" lace ribbon
1 ea. 20 mm pearl bead
1 ea. 12" tinsel stem
3 spring type clothespins
tacky craft glue

1 Cut the tinsel stem into two pieces, one 7" long and one 5" long. Bend the 5" piece into a circle to make the halo, leaving a 1 1/2" stem on the end.

2 Cut the ribbon into two pieces 5" long for the wings and one piece 10" long for the dress. Fold the 10" piece up into 1/2" accordion pleats. Clip a clothespin onto one end of the ribbon to hold the folds together while you continue.

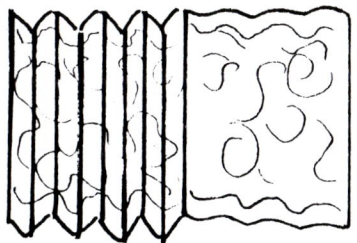

3 Fold a 5" piece of ribbon up into 1/2" pleats and clip a clothespin to the midpoint of the ribbon. Repeat for the second 5" piece of ribbon.

4 Carefully remove the clothespins as you place the midpoints of the 5" pieces on both sides of the 10" piece. They should be 3/4" from the end of the 10" piece.

5 Wrap the 7" length of tinsel stem around all three pieces of ribbon to make a belt and twist the ends of the stem together at the back.

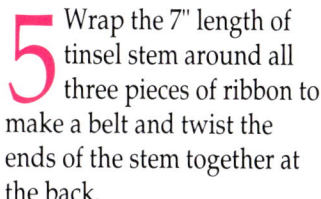

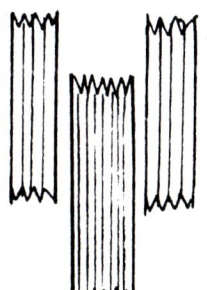

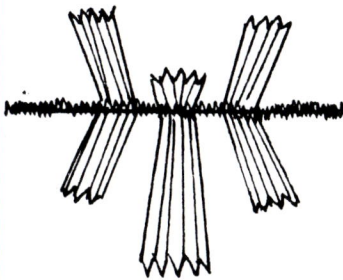

6 Stick the 1 1/2" stem of the halo down through the hole of the pearl bead to make the head. Bend the halo down on top of the head.

7 Glue the end of the stem down into the top of the dress. The stem ends on the back of the angel can be used to wire the angel onto a wreath, garland or tree.

| LEVEL: 2 |
| TIME: 20 min. |
| COST: $1.50 |

RIBBON SOAP HOLDER

Materials:
1 ea. 2" metal ring
12" length of 3" wide lace ribbon
18" length of 1-1/4" wide lace ribbon
5 ea. small silk flowers, assorted colors
glue (see page 3)

1 Cut one end of each piece of ribbon into two points. This will be the bottom end of the holder.

2 Glue the 1-1/4" wide ribbon down the middle of the 3" wide ribbon, making a loop in the 1-1/4" ribbon that is large enough to hold a bar of soap. Glue the back side of the loop down onto the holder.

3 At the top end of the ribbon, fold the two sides in and then slide them through the ring. Fold 1" of the end of the ribbon over and glue it to the back of the holder.

4 Glue the silk flowers to front the holder, just under the ring. Slide a bar of soap through the loop.

This year you'll know just what to get for Grandma... and don't forget to tell her you made it yourself!

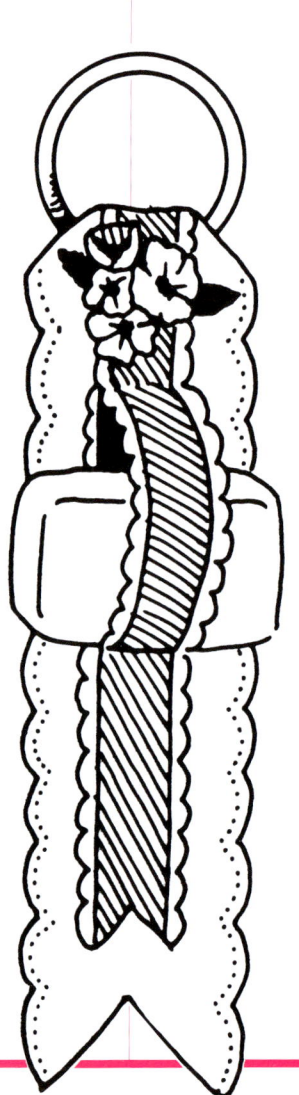

LEVEL: 2
TIME: 20 min.
COST: $ 1.50

RIBBON AND FEATHER MASK

Materials:
1 ea. plain eye mask
5 yds. of 1-1/4" iridescent plastic ribbon
14" length of sequins by the yard
assorted marabou and peacock feathers
1 ea. 3 mm pearl spray
glue (see page 3)

1 From the ribbon cut 30 pieces 1-1/4" long. Cut one end of each piece into a point. Save these small pieces for around the eyes and nose.

2 Cut the remaining ribbon into 2" pieces and trim one end of each of these pieces to a point.

3 Glue a row of these pieces around the outer edge of the mask. Glue on a second row of ribbon pieces about an inch in from the first row so that the bottom edges of the previous row are covered up. Continue gluing rows of the pieces of ribbon, using the smaller ones as you work around the eyes and nose, until the entire mask is covered by the pieces of ribbon. Let the mask dry completely.

4 Glue feathers to the inside top edge of the mask. Snip the pearl spray into individual strands and glue a few into the feathers. Outline the eye holes with the sequins.

Note: Use caution when wearing a mask because of reduced visibility. Materials used to create your mask may be flammable, so avoid open flames such as a candle or a lighter while wearing your mask.

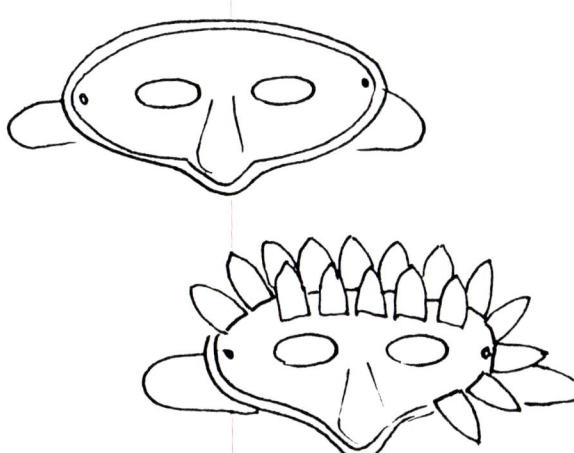

LEVEL: 3
TIME: 2 sessions, 60 min. each if using tacky craft glue. 60 min. if using a glue gun.
COST: $ 5.00

WOVEN RIBBON BARRETTE

Materials:
1 ea. metal barrette with a slot in the middle
1 yard ea. of two colors of 1/8" woven edge satin ribbon
12 ea. 4 mm faceted beads

1. Slide the two lengths of ribbon halfway through the barrette and tie them together in a knot at the closed end of the barrette.

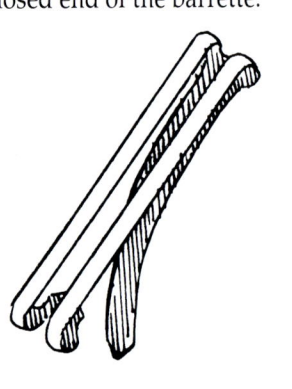

2. There are now four strands of ribbon, one strand each of the two colors on each side of the barrette. Open the barrette to make weaving the ribbon easier. Starting with one of the strands on the left side, thread the ribbon down through the slot and over to the right side. Thread the same colored ribbon on the right side down through the slot and over to the left side.

3. Pick up the second colored ribbon on the left side and thread it down through the slot and over to the right side. Thread the same colored ribbon on the right side down through the slot and over to the left side. The colors will alternate and create a V pattern down the length of the barrette. Repeat the steps until the barrette is completely covered.

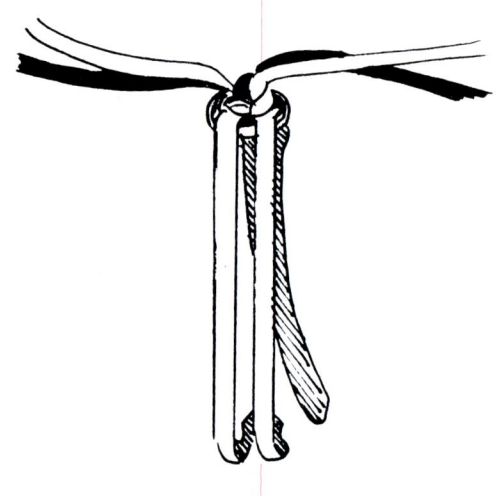

4. Tie the four strands together in a tight knot at the open end of the barrette. Place a dab of glue on the knot to secure it. Trim the ends of the ribbon to a long point and slide three 4 mm faceted beads onto each strand. Tie a knot in each ribbon to keep the beads from sliding off.

LEVEL: 2
TIME: 30 min.
COST: $ 1.35

PLASTIC CANVAS RAINBOW

Materials:
1/2 of a 3" plastic canvas circle
1 yd. ea. of five colors of embroidery floss
1 ea. #16 tapestry needle
small piece of light weight wire

1 Cut the plastic canvas circle in half. One piece will have a smooth cut edge and the other piece will have a jagged edge. You can use either piece to make the rainbow. Cut out the inside four rows of holes from the canvas, leaving five rows to be woven.

2 Cut one of the pieces of embroidery floss into three 12" lengths. Combine the three pieces and thread them all onto the needle at the same time. Weave the floss through one of the rows of the canvas.

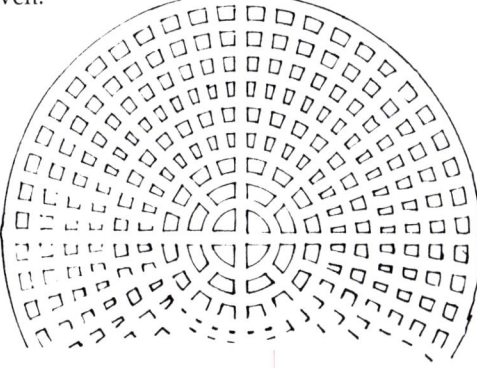

3 The floss at both ends of the canvas should be the same length. Cut a second piece of floss into three pieces and weave it through another row of the canvas. Repeat the process with each of the remaining pieces of floss until all the rows of the canvas are filled up. Separate the ends of the floss with a comb to make a fringe.

4 Attach a small piece of light weight wire to the top of the rainbow to make a hanger. A nice variation uses 18" lengths of 1/8" ribbon in rainbow colors instead of the floss.

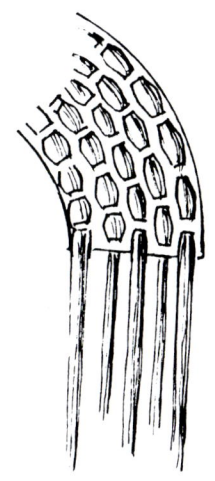

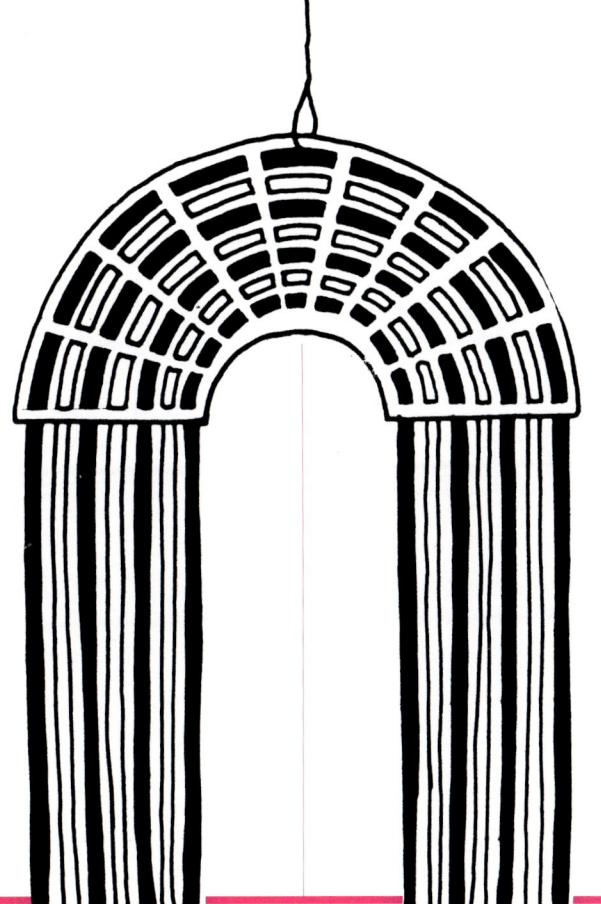

LEVEL: 1
TIME: 30 min.
COST: $ .55

PLASTIC LACING KEY RING/ ZIPPER PULL

Materials:
1 ea. 1" key ring or lanyard hook
1 ea. 9 mm split ring (for key ring)
2 ft. ea. of two colors of plastic lacing
2-6 pony beads or heart beads, assorted colors

1 If the plastic lacing is curly, place it in warm water for a few seconds to straighten out.

2 If making a key ring, attach the split ring to the key ring. The split ring looks just like the key ring, only smaller. It will let the braid slide around the key ring without getting caught up on the key ring. Slide both pieces of lacing halfway through the split ring to create four strands of lacing. Thread all four strands through some of the pony or heart beads. The number and color of beads that you use is up to you. Pull the beads up tight against the ring.

3 Turn the beads so that you are looking where the four strands come out of the beads. Spread out the four strands so they are evenly spaced. Label the four strands #1, #2, #3 and #4.

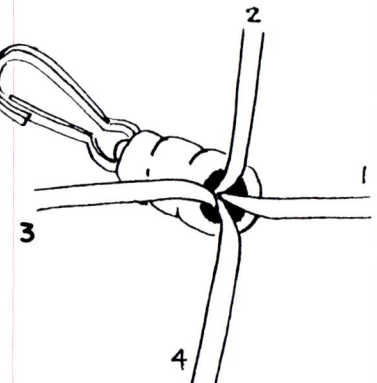

4 Pick up strand #1 and place it on top of strand #2, leaving a small loop in strand #1.

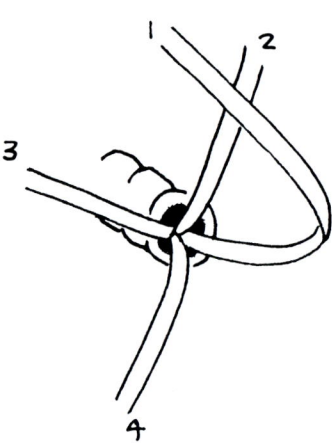

5 Pick up strand #2 and place it on top of strand #3. Pick up strand #3 and place it on top of strand #4. Pick up strand #4 and slide it down through the loop that you left in #1.

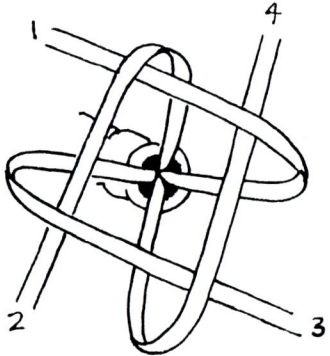

6 Pull evenly on all four strands until all the slack has been pulled out. You will see the lacing form a small square as you pull tightly on the four strands. You have just completed one step.

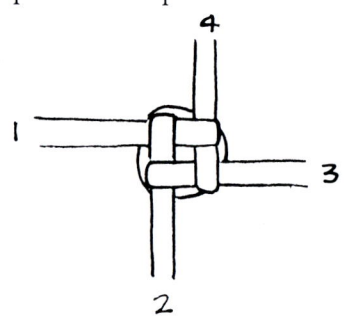

7 Pick up one of the strands, it does not matter which one, and re-label it #1. Re-label the others #2, #3 and #4. Again place #1 over #2, #2 over #3, #3 over #4, and #4 down through the loop in #1. Repeat this step over and over, moving in the same direction. It does not matter which strand you pick up and re-label #1 for each new step. Repeat this step about twenty four times, or about 2", for a key ring.

8 To make a zipper pull, follow the above directions but slide the lacing through a lanyard hook instead of a split ring and only braid for 1 1/2".

9 You will be able to create different braided patterns in your project with two methods: method one is to change the order of the colors of the lacing at the very beginning of the project. Method two is to change directions in braiding after each completed step. First try a project where the colors are in order. An example is pink, pink, blue, blue. Then, try a project where the colors alternate, as in pink, blue, pink, blue. Both projects will have a swirl pattern, but they will be slightly different. If you always move in the same direction your braid will be round. If you do one step in one direction followed by one step in the opposite direction, your braid will be square. When doing a square braid, you will get different patterns by changing the order of the colors of the lacing.

10 After you have completed your braiding, whichever pattern or shape you have decided to do, thread a few more pony or heart beads onto all four strands. Pull them up tight against the last braid. Tie an overhand knot with all four strands just underneath the last bead. Add a dab of cement at the knot. Trim off the excess lacing about 1 1/2" from the knot.

11 Helpful hints: If your braiding doesn't look right, it probably isn't. Check your work for a mistake. For best looking results, keep the lacing flat while you braid. Braiding is easiest when you hold the project between two fingers in the palm of one hand while you braid with the other hand. Keep your work tight for best results.

LEVEL: 3
TIME: 40 min.
COST: approx. $.35

PLASTIC CANVAS JEWELRY HOLDER

Materials:
6" x 8" piece of colored plastic needlepoint canvas
1 yd. each of five colors of plastic lacing
sharp craft knife
glue (see page 3)

1 Have an adult cut out the openings in the plastic canvas with the knife. Needlepoint canvas is usually worked with yarn and a needle. By using plastic lacing, you do not need a needle and you do not need to buy full skeins of yarn.

2 With the plastic lacing, outline the outer edges and the openings with a simple continental needlepoint stitch. This stitch, also called a half cross stitch, is made by coming up through a hole in the canvas and back down through the hole that is one space up and one space over from the first hole. Don't tie knots with the lacing.

3 When you need to fasten the ends, start the piece of lacing by leaving a 3/4" tail hanging out the back of the canvas. As you do the first four stitches, catch the tail underneath the stitches on the back to hold it in place.

4 When ending a piece of lacing, tuck the end of the lacing under four stitches on the back. Don't pull the lacing up tight on these last four stitches until after you have worked the end of the lacing under them. You may even want to use a large needle, #13 size, to make a space under the stitches for the lacing to fit through.

5 After you have finished outlining the edges and openings, cut three pieces of lacing each 12" long to make a hanger for your jewelry holder. Have someone hold the ends for you and tie a braid for 7". Lace the ends of the braid through the top edge of the canvas and tie each end into a knot. Place a dab of glue on the knot to secure it. Trim off the excess lacing from the braid.

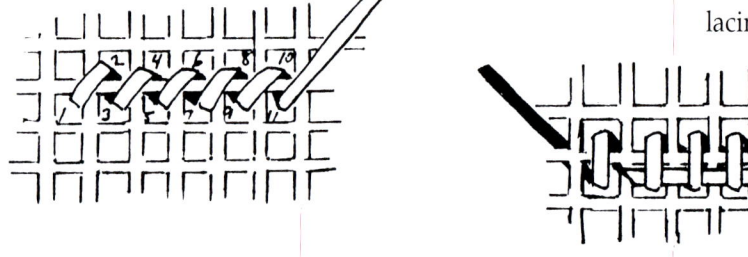

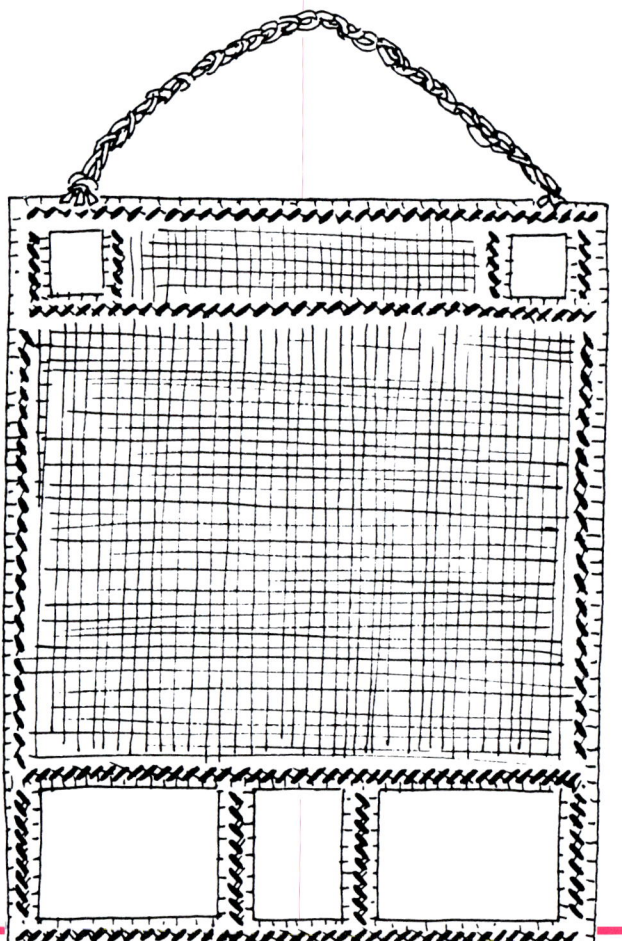

LEVEL: 2
TIME: 90 min.
COST: $ 1.00

T-SHIRT SPONGE PAINTING

Materials:
pre-cut sponge stamps or 2 medium store bought sponges
1/4" flat bristle brush
fabric paints, assorted colors
pre-washed t-shirt

1 Place the t-shirt over a piece of plastic covered cardboard. Cut sponges into interesting shapes with a pair of scissors.

2 Place some fabric paint on a plate and dip a sponge into the paint. You can also brush the paints onto the sponge to use a couple of colors on the sponge at the same time. If the paint is very thick, thin it a bit with some water.

3 Dip the sponges into the paint and press them onto the fabric. Don't try to cover up the texture of the sponge, but rather let it become part of the design.

4 Sponge painting can also be combined with masking tape painting and stencil painting for interesting results. When the paint is dry, heat set it if your paints require it.

ABOUT FABRIC PAINTING

There are many kinds of fabric painting to choose from at your local craft store. Some paints need to be heat set with an iron and a pressing cloth to set their color after they have dried. Others should not be ironed at all. Be sure to read the instructions that come with the paints.

No matter which kind of paint you choose, all new fabric should be washed and dried, without fabric softener, before you paint on it. Washing the fabric first removes the sizing, allowing the paint to adhere better to it.

Before you begin painting, stretch the fabric over plastic covered cardboard. Hold the fabric tight with masking tape. If you are painting on a piece of clothing, slide a piece of plastic covered cardboard up inside to keep the paint from soaking through to the back of the clothing.

Even though all fabric paints are made to be washable after they dry, your painting will look better if you wash your clothing in a short or gentle cycle and dry on low heat. You may wear your newly painted clothing as soon as the paint is dry. However, it is best to wait a couple of days before you wash it for the first time. This allows thicker paints to bond to the fabric.

LEVEL: 2
TIME: 6 min.
COST: $ 5.00

T-SHIRT MASKING TAPE PAINTING

Materials:
1" wide masking tape
metallic water-based fabric paints, two or three colors
white pearl and gold glitter paint in squeeze bottles
1/2" flat bristle paint brush
pre-washed t-shirt

1. Pre-wash your t-shirt. After it has dried, slide it over a plastic covered piece of cardboard. The fabric should be pulled tight across the cardboard.

2. Outline different shapes on your t-shirt with 1" wide masking tape. Place the tape on your fabric to form squares, triangles, stars and rectangles. Press firmly down on the edges of the tape. Because the masking tape will keep the edges crisp and straight, the inside areas of the designs will be easy to paint with the metallic paints.

3. Brush paint on in an even coat. Sometimes a second coat is needed when using glitters.

4. Dry the painted areas for a couple of minutes with a hair dryer before removing the masking tape. Do not leave the tape on too long or the tape will be hard to remove.

5. After the metallic paint has dried and the tape has been removed, add zigzags and dots to the shapes with the white pearl and gold glitter paint. You can wear the after the paint has dried but wait a few days before first washing it.

There's no limit to what you can come up with on T-shirts like these... get colorful!

LEVEL: 1
TIME: 60 min.
COST: $ 3.00 worth of paint per shirt

T-SHIRT FABRIC STENCILING

Materials:
Pre-cut plastic stencil
stencil brush to fit the size stencil you are using
water based fabric paints, colors of your choice
masking tape
pre-washed t-shirt

1. Pre-wash your t-shirt. Slide the shirt over a piece of plastic-covered cardboard. Tape the stencil onto your fabric. Tape off areas you want to paint later with other colors.

2. Dip the stencil brush into the paint. Rub most of the paint off onto a paper towel before you start painting. This keeps the paint from bleeding under the stencil. Brush the paint into the fabric using a circular motion. Start with light pressure and increase the pressure as you want more paint on the fabric.

3. When you have completed all areas of the first color, remove the tape and place it over the areas you just painted to protect them. Wash the brush out and dry it thoroughly before going to the next color. Excess water will dilute the paint and make it bleed under the stencil. Paint all the areas of the next color.

4. Continue the above steps until the entire stencil has been painted. Remove the stencil and wash it and the brush with soap and water. When the paint is completely dry, heat set it if your paints require it. Wash and dry according to the directions on the paint label.

Create your own designs!

LEVEL: 3
TIME: 60 min.
COST: $ 3.00

CHRISTMAS SNOW SCENE IN JAR

Materials:
- 1 clean jar and lid, 8-12 oz. size
- 1 small plastic lid, from a salad dressing bottle
- gold spray paint
- plastic santa or figures of your choice
- 1/2 tsp. diamond dust
- low heat glue gun or waterproof cement

1. Spray paint the jar lid with a couple of light coats of gold paint. Let the paint dry completely.

2. Glue the small plastic lid down into the jar lid to create a raised platform for the santa to stand on. Glue the santa on top of the platform. Let the glue dry completely.

3. Fill the jar with water. Lower the santa down into the jar to force out the excess water. Pour out a little more water. When the jar lid is on, you want the water level to be about 1/4" below the jar lid so that the glue or cement does not get wet while it is drying. Remove the santa. Dry off the jar lid and the rim of the jar.

4. Stir the diamond dust into the water.

5. Squeeze out a generous amount of glue around the inside edge of the jar lid. Lower the santa back down into the water, being careful not to get water on the glue. Screw the jar lid on tight.

6. If you are using cement, leave the jar upright for several hours before turning it upside down. The diamond dust may float at the top of the water for a few days until it becomes saturated. It will then settle slowly to the bottom of the jar whenever you shake your snow scene.

LEVEL: 2
TIME: 2 sessions, 20 min ea.
COST: approx. $2.00

SNOWMAN IN A JAR

Materials:
1 ea. 23 mm black plastic top hat
2 ea. black 4 mm beads (eyes)
small piece of orange non-hardening, oil base clay (carrot nose)
1 ea. small jar with a lid, 6-8 oz. size
1/4" tsp. diamond dust
low heat glue gun or waterproof cement

1. Roll a small piece of orange clay in your fingers to form a carrot.

2. Lightly press some lines into the clay to make ridges on the carrot. Fill the jar up to 1/4" from the top with water and stir in the diamond dust. Drop in the two beads, the carrot and the top hat.

3. Dry off the rim of the jar and the inside of the lid. Squeeze out a generous amount of glue or cement along the inside edge of the lid. Screw the lid down tight.

4. Wait for the glue to set up completely before you shake the jar.

What a cute idea! Now you can keep Frosty all year long... even in warm weather! Just give him a shake once in awhile for good luck.

LEVEL: 2
TIME: 20 min.
COST: approx. $.50

EMBOSSING WITH POT PIE PANS & TOOLING COPPER

Materials:
pot pie pan with plain bottom or 36 g. tooling copper
hammer
small nail
piece of scrap wood
stack of newspaper
dried up ball point pen

1 Cut out the bottom circle of the pot pie pan or 36g. tooling copper. Copper circles should be cut with a pair of old craft scissors. The edges are sharp, so be careful not to cut yourself on the edges or corners.

2 Trace a pattern onto the circle. Place the circle on top of a stack of newspaper and re-draw the design with the dried up pen. Turn the circle over and draw new lines right next to, but not on top of, the first lines. Continue drawing, first on one side and then the other, until the design is completed.

3 To add some punch work to your embossing, place the copper on top of a piece scrap wood and tap small holes in it with a hammer and nail. Tap a hole in the top of the circle and thread ribbon through to make a hanger.

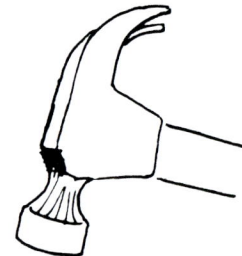

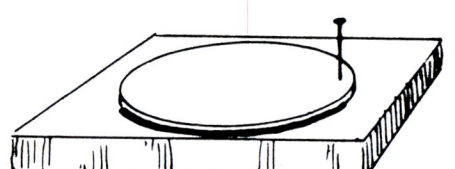

4 You can make the copper change color by putting pieces of the copper in the oven at 350° for 10 minutes. It will turn dark orange, pink, and then gray. Burnish the copper with fine steel wool to bring out some of the original copper color. If you soak the copper in vinegar it will completely turn back to the original color.

LEVEL: 1
TIME: 20 min.
COST: approx. $ .45

FURNACE FILTER ORNAMENTS

Materials:
furnace filter
clear contact paper
small silk flowers
small photo
10" length of metallic cord

1 Cut out the honey-combed piece of metal from the filter using craft scissors. Once you have decided how many circles you will need for your project, cut out the piece from the metal.

2 Place a piece of contact paper that is slightly larger than the metal on a flat surface, sticky side up. Lay the metal on top of the contact paper with the good side of the metal facing up. Cut out a small photo and place it in one of the circles.

3 Cut the silk flowers off the stems. You want the flowers to be as flat as possible so pull off the plastic centers if they are thick. Trim pieces of leaves to fit inside the circles. Use an extra circle to see how much room you have. Place the bits of leaves and the flowers on top of the sticky contact paper.

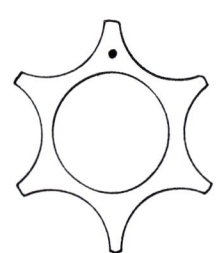

4 When all the circles are filled up, place another piece of contact paper, sticky side down, on top of the metal. Lay the contact paper down carefully so you don't trap air bubbles or wrinkle it up.

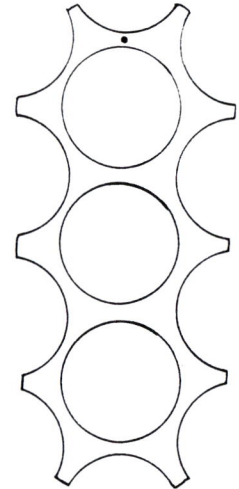

5 Trim off the excess contact paper by taking little cuts with the scissors along the outer edge of the metal.

6 Make a hole with a small nail and hammer in the top of the filter piece. Attach the metallic cord to make a hanger.

LEVEL: 2
TIME: 40 min.
COST: approx. $.45